Durga Puja

The book is an introduction to Durga Puja, the grandest festival in eastern India, a celebration that provides a glimpse into the rich cultural heritage of Bengal. It is also a ready reckoner of all aspects of the Puja — its mythical origins, its socio-cultural evolution, its economic ramifications and its elaborate rituals. Spiced up with anecdotes and trivia collected from journals and newspapers from the 19th century to the present day, it is a compendium of knowledge associated with the worship of the Mother Goddess, one of the oldest surviving Hindu traditions.

Sudeshna Banerjee is a journalist. She has been writing on Durga Puja for years and has also produced the script for a documentary film on the festival. A keen traveller, photographer and collector of stamps and coins, she lives with her family in Calcutta.

Durga Puja

Yesterday, Today & Tomorrow

Sudeshna Banerjee

Rupa & Co

To the Mother
and my mother
for making me write this book

Copyright © Sudeshna Banerjee 2004

First Published 2004
Second Impression 2006

Published by
Rupa & Co
7/16, Ansari Road, Daryaganj,
New Delhi 110 002

Sales Centres:

Allahabad Bangalore Chandigarh Chennai
Hyderabad Jaipur Kathmandu
Kolkata Mumbai Pune

Photographs by
Vishakha Karnani, Rashbehari Das and Sudeshna Banerjee

Typeset in 11 pts. Caxton by
Nikita Overseas Pvt. Ltd.
1410 Chiranjiv Tower
43 Nehru Place
New Delhi 110 019

Printed in India by
Saurabh Printers Pvt. Ltd.
A-16 Sector-IV
Noida 201 301

Contents

Preface

Durga Puja seems an all-too-familiar subject to write a book on as people from this part of the world get to live this gorgeous festival every year. Yet the intimacy perhaps fogs the questioning eye and the habit of taking the big picture for granted makes one unmindful of the smaller details.

I have been lucky in being born in the Puja heartland, and the high point of my childhood autumns used to be enthusiastic performances with the *kanshor-ghanta* (a percussion instrument comprising a bell metal plate and a stick) as accompanist to the *dhaki* (drummer) at the local community puja pandal in Ranaghat, Nadia, about 74 km away from Calcutta.

I have been even luckier in getting the chance to prepare myself for a conscious distancing that is vital to arouse the queries that lie buried under years of unquestioning experience. Writing a script for a documentary film on Durga Puja and researching the subject for a series of festival-special articles for *The Telegraph* gave me the wherewithal to embark on this project.

The book seeks to be an overview of the transmutation of the most spectacular phenomenon to emerge out of Bengal and spread its wings across the globe in the last century.

A store of information to help the researcher, a ready reckoner for the uninitiated, a collection of unknown answers to questions never asked for those who grew up with the Puja, like myself, and entertainment for everyone—this, in a nutshell, is what the book is. It does not pretend to be a scholarly work on the anthropological origin and evolution of the autumnal ritual.

And the product would not have reached the press in the present form without the help of:

- Prof. Kalyani Ghosh, who guided me through the birthpangs and held my hand firmly even in moments of uncertainty and despair
- Prof. Supriya Chaudhuri, who edited a major portion of the book with an affectionate teacher's care
- Sumit Das Gupta, who gave me ample leave, latitude and support to write the book
- Dr Achintya Mukhopadhyay, who kept my morale high and did an engineer brother's best to plug the loopholes that stayed in the writing
- Sarottama Majumdar, who proved once again what friends are for by taking part in many a brainstorming session and offering her scholarly comments
- Dipayan Chatterjee, who provided me with encouragement when I needed it most
- Soma Biswas, who, faithful as ever, fought with Time to provide me with a store of beautiful sketches at a short notice
- Dipendra Chattopadhyay, who turned reporter and photographer in New York for this book's sake
- the Chatterjeas, Sunil Kumar, Tara, Arkadev, Bhargabi and my dear friend and refuge Surjamukhi, who were all there, like my own family, to help me out in whichever way

- Purba Sengupta and Narayan Sanyal who spared time to answer all my queries
- Vishakha Karnani who became a friend, with and without the camera
- Somdatta Ghosh, Dr Damayanti Datta, Reshmi Sengupta, Dr Barnita Bagchi and Tanmoy Bhattacharya who offered advice whenever asked for
- Biswajit Matilal, Alok Krishna Deb, Michael Bose, Pradip Ghosh, Samir Roychowdhury, Nijan Dey Chowdhury, Pankaj Banerjee, Arijit Roy Chowdhury and the Belur Math authorities who helped me gather quality visual material and reference books
- the image-makers, decorators and weapon-suppliers of Kumortuli, the priests in Calcutta and Ranaghat, and the puja organisers and theme-makers who shared their knowledge and experiences with me
- Lila Mukherjee and Dr Sumita Mukhopadhyay who remained, as ever, my loyal support block
- my mother Krishna Banerjee who turned into my assistant for the project and father Manindra Nath Banerjee who has built up a treasure trove of a library at home

I end this personal note with a story that I heard from a British friend, Heather Nice, who had spent years in Calcutta. One Puja, she took some European acquaintances on a pandal-hopping trip. At the entrance of a south Calcutta pandal, they paused wondering whether they would be allowed in. "Suddenly we noticed that a street-side music band had stopped playing and the members were whispering amongst themselves pointing at us. That made us so nervous that we told ourselves, 'We shouldn't be here. Let's clear out'. The next moment they had broken into the opening bars of *Que sera sera*, which perhaps was the only Western tune they knew."

This warm inclusiveness is what Durga Puja is about,
and please god, may it stay this way.

Calcutta, March 2004

1

Mythical Roots

Durga, the demon-slaying goddess, comes on a visit every year for four days to fill our home and hearth with an abundance of happiness. She is accompanied by her divine children—daughters Laxmi and Saraswati and sons Kartik and Ganesha.

A consort of Lord Shiva and an icon of female power, she finds mention in the Vedas, the Puranas, the epics and a variety of other religious texts. Across the country, she is worshipped under various appellations, in different forms and usually alone. She is Amba or Ambika in Kashmir and the Deccan region, Hingala or Rudrani in Gujarat, Kalyani in Karnataka, Uma in Mithila, Bhavani in Rajasthan, Kanyakumari in the southern-most tip of the country, Katyayani in Vrindavan, Haripriya in Hardwar, Bheemadevi in Himachal, Vaishnodevi in Jammu, Vindhyabashini in Vindhyachal, Vimala in Puri, Kamakhya in Kamrup, Jaidurga in Baidyanath... The list goes on. A *vrat* called Navratri is observed with much fanfare around the period of Durga Puja in many regions. The Dussehra festival in north and west India takes place on the last day of the Puja, also celebrating the victory of good over evil. But nowhere has the worship of the mother goddess come to exercise such an all-pervasive influence over the collective imagination and life of a people.

The form in which Durga is worshipped in the annual festival is derived from the saga of King Surath, who is said to have carried out the first Durga Puja on earth. The *Markandeyapurana* narrates how Surath had retired to the forest in despair, having lost his kingdom and the love of his kin. There he met Samadhi, a man from a lower caste, who was in no less anguish. The two chanced upon the abode of the sage Medha in the forest. According to the sage's advice, they went to a river bank and moulded the goddess in clay. Together, they worshipped her until one day she appeared before them and offered a boon. Samadhi sought deliverance from the cycle of life and death while Surath asked for his lost kingdom. Durga obliged both and disappeared.

Time of worship: Autumn over spring

Durga Puja, as we know it, has shifted slot in the seasonal calendar. While the worship by King Surath took place in spring, today it is an autumnal affair. For that, one has to look at a post-Valmiki[1] later-day version of the epic, the *Ramayana*, authored by the Bengali poet, Krittivasa.

Rama, while fighting with Ravana to retrieve wife Sita from the abductor's grip, invoked the Goddess in autumn. Since Ravana was a devotee of Durga, Rama was advised to seek her blessings before going for direct combat against the king of the monsters. After three days of worship, as Rama readied his offerings, he suddenly noticed one of the

108 blue lotuses essential for the worship missing. Desperate to complete his puja, he notched an arrow to his bow and aimed at one of his eyes, which were said to be as beautiful as lotuses. Just as he was about to shoot, Durga appeared, appeased by his devotion, and stopped him from sacrificing his eye. It was she who had hidden one of the flowers to test Rama. She promised to aid him in the war. A great battle followed and Ravana was killed.

In some accounts, it is Brahma who invoked Durga to secure her aid for Rama. After all, Rama was on the gods' side, being an earthly incarnation of Vishnu. Brahma found the goddess in the guise of a beautiful girl, asleep on a leafy branch of a *bel* (woodapple) tree on earth. The goddess awoke at his invocation and promised to empower Rama's bow on the seventh day of the full moon fortnight so that Ravana would be killed at the conjunction of the eighth and ninth days of the fortnight.

After Ravana's death, Brahma, along with all the gods, worshipped her. This custom has been retained in the Pujas, with the last day of the festival being named Vijaya Dashami, the victorious tenth day, a celebration of the victory of Rama over Ravana, or good over evil.

The time of Rama's worship is considered to be unseasonable. A year in the human life amounts to a day on the divine calendar. Six months of the year is a day for the gods while the other six is night. Spring is part of the divine day, while autumn falls in the nocturnal half.[2] Durga stays awake in spring and there is no need to invoke her in the vernal version of the puja (which is not much in practice today). But in autumn, she has to be woken up from sleep before the worship can start.

In all these myths about the evolution of her worship, Durga appears alone. The mother and wife are identities that she took on over time, and are typical of the eastern part of India where other gods and goddesses have become part of her entourage as her children. The accumulation of a cluster of deities to her side approximating a familial structure and, more significantly, the appropriation of a warrior-goddess as a daughter of the land are phenomena unique to the region north of the Bay of Bengal.

Genesis of the gods

Each of the figures in Durga's entourage has a story of origin. Often, there is more than one account of the birth. Sometimes, for the whole picture to emerge, pieces have to be stitched together from a number of myths revolving round separate gods or goddesses. This is because in Hindu mythology, divine power is manifest in myriad figures with different names. Individual myths emphasise one aspect of the god or goddess while assuming it is linked to many others. The details vary from region to region and from text to text.

Durga: The demon-slayer

Durga derives her name from her identity as the slayer of the demon Durgo. This demon was wreaking havoc on heaven and earth. Shiva, the trident-bearing Supreme Destroyer, was helpless against him as Durgo was invincible against all males. At Shiva's request, his consort Parvati assumed the form of a warrior and killed the demon.[3] The connection to Parvati places Durga in a familial context and provides a vital clue to why a martial goddess is worshipped as a mother and wife.

Parvati, after all, is the daughter of the Himalayas who gained Shiva's love after long penance and married him against her mother's wishes. It is this daughter who returns to the lap of the Himalayas every year with her children from her divine abode on Mt Kailash.

She is again a goddess of vegetation (as symbolised by the Nabapatrika, a collection of nine branches of plants, kept to the right of Ganesha during the worship), returning every year with promise of a good harvest. In *Markandeyapurana*, after demon-king Shumba falls, Durga departs with the promise that if crops failed she would return as Shakambhari and nourish the world with vegetation.

The epic, *Mahabharata,* describes Durga as one who ends all miseries (*durgati-nashini*). In *Devipurana*, she is also the protector of fortresses (*durgo* means a fortress in Sanskrit).

The form in which Durga is portrayed in the annual festival derives from another myth. Mahishasura, the buffalo-demon, once prayed long and hard to Brahma, the Father of Creation. Satisfied, the god appeared before the king of the nether world and offered him a boon. Mahishasura sought to be immortal. When this was refused, he thought up the next best option—that he die only at the hand of a woman. After all, what risk would he, an intrepid warrior, stand from a frail female! Armed with this confidence, he set off to conquer the universe. First, he took over earth and then marched with his army towards heaven. The war raged for a thousand years and the demons were victorious. The gods were driven out of heaven and flocked to Lord Shiva for protection. As Shiva listened to their tale of woe, a divine effulgence emanated from his face. The other gods too emitted a similar glow. This energy combined to take a 1,000-armed towering female form (see box). Jewellery and gems from Kshirod Sagar, the mythical sea of milk, were brought to dress her up with earrings, rings, bangles, necklaces and anklets. The gods, then, created replicas of their own weapons

Divine conception

The glow emanating from each of the gods shaped a distinct portion of the divine figure.

Shiva>>face; Yama, the god of death>>hair; Vishnu>>arms; Chandra, the moon-god>>breasts; Indra, the thunder-god>>loin; Varuna, the sea-god>>thighs and shank; Earth>>hips; Brahma>>feet; Surya, the sun-god>>fingers of the feet; Ashtabashu, the eight demigods>>fingers of the hand; Kubera, the god of wealth>> nose; Prajapati, Brahma's ten grandsons>>teeth; Agni, the fire god>>three eyes; Sandhya, the evening goddess>>brows; Vayu, the god of wind>>ears.

and armed her (see box). Himalaya, the king of the mountains, gifted her a lion which she took as her mount.

Adorned in finery and armed to the teeth, Durga let out a roar and headed for Mahishasura's palace. Such was the impact of the sound that it unleashed cyclones in the sea and landslides in the mountains. Mahishasura rushed out to check the cause of the uproar. But on seeing Durga, he burst out laughing. This infuriated Durga even further. She reminded the demon-king of his vulnerability, and urged him to battle. As Mahishasura summoned his army, Durga exhaled deeply. Immediately, thousands of soldiers were produced to fight on her side. The demon, who could take on the guise of any animal, first assumed his favourite form, that of the buffalo. It trampled on hundreds and injured hundreds more with the lashing of its tail. Durga threw a lasso at the raging animal. To slip out of the noose, Mahishasura transformed himself into a lion. But Durga soon chopped off its head with a sword.

Gifts from the gods

Shiva>>trident; Vishnu>>discus; Vayu>> bow and quiver; Agni>>mace; Mahakaal (Time)>>falchion; Yama>> shield*; Varuna>>Nagpash**; Indra >>elephant goad and bell; Viswakarma, the divine craftsman>>axe.

*In some accounts, Yama's gift is Kaldanda, his staff, the touch of which spells death.
**Nagpash: A missile from which snakes spring forth and fasten the enemy in a poisonous embrace.

Accounts vary from scripture to scripture. In some, the catalogue includes a garland of beads and a water-pot from Brahma and thunder from Indra.

The demon king waged war in his own form for some time before metamorphosing into an elephant. The elephant attacked Durga's mount, the lion. Durga immediately cut off its trunk with her sword. At this, the elephant gave up its form and turned to a buffalo. As the buffalo raged across Creation, the Goddess raised a cup of wine to her lips and glared at the animal with blood-shot eyes. "Roar as you please, you foolish beast. When I destroy you, the gods will make more noise in celebration."

The buffalo, which was hurling trees and mountains at her, now sped towards her, neck craned and horns pointed. Durga leapt on the creature and cut off its head in one fell blow. Mahishasura tried making his way out of the creature's body but Durga was ready. The divine trident pierced the demon's chest. This is the moment that is frozen in the images worshipped every autumn.

Kartik: The warlord

Kartik, the general of the divine army, the handsome bachelor god, is shown in some accounts as the off-spring of the union of Agni, the fire god, and Ganga, the river goddess. Ganga failed to go through with the pregnancy and expelled Agni's burning seed from her body. The seed became a baby and was deposited on her banks from where six *krittika*s, or demigoddesses, rescued it.

But the more popular myth, based on *Skandapurana*, makes Kartik a son to Shiva and Parvati. Once Surapadma, the demon king, became powerful by Shiva's boon. He defeated and enslaved the gods. The humiliated gods flocked to Kailash, Shiva's abode. Shiva took pity on them. After all, it was according to his boon, that none but he could defeat Surapadma. He transformed himself into a six-headed figure and produced six glowing masses of light.

A divine pronouncement followed—the child born out of the glow would be the saviour of the gods. Shiva instructed that the balls of light be transported to Ganga, the river goddess, who would deposit them in the bulrushes near Mt Uday. As soon as the glowing balls reached the base of the mountain, they metamorphosed into six new-born babies.

They were spotted by six *krittika*s, who adopted them. But when the gods reached the riverbank, the babies became a six-headed boy. Shiva named the boy after each of the agents who played a part in its creation. The name by which he is known today is Kartik, a derivation of Kartikeya, son of the *krittika*s.

Soon after, Kartik was sent to war armed with Shiva's spear. He defeated the demon Surapadma in battle. In the throes of death, Surapadma expressed repentance and sought his protection. Kartik forgave him and accepted him as his mount, the peacock.

Ganesha: The giver of success

According to *Shivapurana*, Ganesha came into being as the result of a domestic squabble between Shiva and Parvati. Shiva let his rowdy followers into Kailash at ungodly hours. Parvati felt she had no privacy. So in consultation with her companions Jaya and Bijaya, she created a boy who would take orders only from her. The boy was put on duty at the gate with instructions to bar everyone.

Soon, Shiva and company arrived but were stopped at the gate by the intrepid boy. They reasoned with him, they pleaded with him, they threatened him—all to no avail. Instead, he beat up Shiva's henchmen, Nandi and Bhringi.

The news of the scuffle soon reached the other gods, who challenged the boy to combat. Yet so successfully did the boy parry the charges that the gods had to resort to mischief. Vishnu engaged him in direct combat while Shiva chopped off his head from behind.

Parvati was overwhelmed with grief at the news of her son's death and wreaked havoc on Creation. In order to propitiate her, Shiva ordered his followers to collect the head of any creature they set eyes on in the northern direction. They came back with the head of a one-tusked elephant. The elephant's head was attached to the torso of the beheaded boy. He sat up and all was well again. Shiva blessed him, saying that he would be worshipped at the start of all rituals and gave him the name Ganesha (lord of the masses).[4]

There is another myth associated with Ganesha's birth, related in *Brahmabaibartapurana*. Shiva and Parvati were childless for a long time. They practised penance for years and after that a son was born to Parvati. There was jubilation at Kailash. All the gods gathered to see the bonny boy and were showering blessings on him. But only Shani or Saturn, the god of misfortune, was staying away from the cradle. He had been cursed by his wife that whatever he laid his eyes on would be destroyed. But Parvati did not know about the curse and the proud mother was highly offended at what she thought was Shani's slighting of her newborn son. At last, Shani was forced to look at the baby, whose head immediately was destroyed under the cold gaze. Parvati was inconsolable. The rest of the story unfolds along similar lines. Vishnu rushed out to the forest with his Sudarshan Chakra, or divine discus. The elephant's head he returned with replaced the boy's.[5]

Saraswati: The goddess of learning

The origin of the *veena*-bearing goddess is not as distinct as that of the other figures. In the Vedas, especially the *Rig Veda*, she is referred to as both a river and a river deity. The Saraswati river was a boundary of Brahmavartta, the home of the early Aryans, and was to them as sacred as the Ganga has been to their descendants. Gradually she became associated with the rites performed on her banks and started being regarded as an influence on the composition of the hymns that were an important part of the rituals. This might have led to her identification with Vak, the goddess of speech.[6] In later mythology she finds mention as the spouse of Brahma and the goddess of wisdom, eloquence and the arts.

The father of the universe prepared himself for Creation and sunk in deep meditation. The sublime quality of his spirit (*sattvaguna*) accumulated in his mind and was emitted from his forehead as Speech or Saraswati. He ordained that she stay on the tip of everyone's tongue and exist on earth as a river. A part of her was also to stay in him.[7]

But, according to another account, she was born so beautiful that the old hoary-headed god immediately desired her. She tried to escape his attentions but wherever she flew, he grew a head in that direction to keep a watch on her. Brahma thus came to have five heads, four on the sides and one on top. Saraswati fled to the forest as a deer and swam into the deep waters as a swan. But there was no escape. Finally she had to yield to his desire.[8]

Laxmi: The goddess of prosperity

During Creation, a beautiful female form emerged from the left side of Paramatma, the Supreme Being. At a command from Paramatma, she split herself into two enchanting figures, both equal in splendour and majesty. One was Laxmi and the other Radha. Both wanted Paramatma as their consort. So he divided himself into the two-armed Krishna and the four-armed Vishnu. While Radha chose Krishna and stayed on earth, Laxmi wedded Vishnu and left for the heavens.[9]

Laxmi has many manifestations. As Swargalaxmi (Laxmi of the heavens), she lived in the palace of Indra, the king of the gods.

One day, the sage Durbasha offered a garland of *parijat*, the heavenly flower, to Indra. The garland had special properties of bearing the essence of Shree, or Fortune. But the king of gods, engaged in the amorous company of the beautiful courtesan Rambha, playfully placed the garland on his mount Airavat's forehead. The tusker straightaway hurled it to the ground and trampled on it. This slight infuriated Durbasha and he cursed Indra that he be rid of his Shree, which was embodied in Laxmi, the goddess of wealth, well-being and prosperity. So Swargalaxmi left the gods and merged with Mahalaxmi, her idealised manifestation in Vaikuntha.

At this, the gods lost their splendour and the universe was cast in gloom. In the midst of this, the demons struck, driving the weakened gods away from heaven.

The gods flocked to Vishnu in despair. Lord Vishnu, the protector of Creation, requested his consort Mahalaxmi, the idealised manifestation of the goddess, to be born as the daughter of Khirod Sagar. The gods were advised to churn the sea and reinstate Laxmi in heaven. Thus started the mammoth operation, for which the gods sought help from the demons, promising them a share of nectar, the immortality potion, which was also resting in the depths.

After the first few churnings that yielded the great poison *holahol* (requiring Lord Shiva to swallow the entire store and rescue the universe from its noxious fumes) and sundry other miraculous items, Laxmi emerged. She chose Vishnu as her consort and settled down in Vaikuntha.

In another account, when Krishna was lost in the ecstasy of a dance in his youth, a figure of supreme beauty emerged at his side. She split herself into Radha and Laxmi. While Radha stayed back on earth with Krishna, Laxmi retired to the heavens to be with Lord Vishnu.

Yet another account describes Laxmi as the product of the union of Sage Bhrigu and his wife Khyati. There is a use of imagery here. Bhrigu denotes a high standing while Khyati is fame. The confluence of the two creates wealth.[10]

Mahishasura: The buffalo-demon

According to the *Bhagabatpurana*, the brothers Rambha and Karambha were both childless. Aspiring for a child, they started a long and rigorous meditation. While Rambha sat amid blazing flames, Karambha immersed himself in neck-deep water. Indra, the king of the gods, became worried at the intensity of their meditation, lest they win the right to rule the heavens by their piety. So he took the garb of a crocodile and devoured Karambha. Rambha went on with his ascetic rites but when nothing yielded fruit, he tried to chop his own head as sacrifice to the fire. This appeased Shiva who appeared and offered Rambha a boon. Rambha prayed that Shiva himself be born as his son in three successive births. The son would be conquerer of the gods, more spirited than fire, celebrated, truthful, long-living, and possessor of all treasure. Shiva agreed and Rambha returned, joyful at having gained immortality through an illustrious line. On the way, he saw a handsome, healthy buffalo. This buffalo was Mahismati, daughter of the sage Biprachitti. A willful girl, she had taken the guise of a buffalo and scared sage Sindhudweep so much that his long meditation was disturbed. The angry sage had cursed Mahismati that she be locked in the buffalo's body. This is the buffalo that Rambha saw wandering in the forest. He fell in love with Mahismati and married her. Mahishasura was the product of their union.

The unity of power

Though Laxmi and Saraswati are seen as two daughters of Durga, there are no specific myths describing them as such, as there are for Ganesha and Kartik. Rather, the scriptures often refer to them as other forms of the one Female Power. 'Shree Shree Chandi', the section of *Markandeyapurana*, which dwells at great length on Durga, sees this power manifest in three faces—Mahakali (the great Kali), Mahalaxmi (the great Laxmi) and Mahasaraswati (the great Saraswati). Here Mahalaxmi is the one who takes on Mahishasura.

That all the female forms are one is clearly stated by the Devi herself in the Shumba-Nishumba myth. Locked in combat with demon-king Shumba, she was conducting raids on the enemy's army in multiple female forms. The demon complained that there was no glory in victory gained with help from so many quarters. She told him that there was no power in the Universe other than her. The demon king beheld with amazement how all the female forms with different appellations and appearances, that were so long waging war separately, melted into her one by one.

Making sense of the mounts

All members of the entourage are accompanied by an animal with which they share symbolic synergy. What the mounts stand for in some cases reinforces the powers of the god and in others complements them to present the deity in greater glory.

Lion: Durga's mount was a gift from Himalayas when she went to war with Mahishasura. It fought ferociously

on its own in the deciding battle. The lion stands for power. In the pose in which she is worshipped, the Devi has her right foot firmly planted on the lion's back. The accent thus is on extreme self-control, which can keep power on a tight leash and prevent it from spilling on to the realms of tyranny.

Owl: The mount of Laxmi is a nightbird. While men are busy with their worldly pursuits through the day, it is deep in a sleep of disinterestedness. It chooses to stay up and meditate in the calm of night, and guard its store of spiritual wealth. The choice of such a mount for the goddess of prosperity sends out the strong message that spiritual attainment is as important as material acquisitions for a person to prosper.

Swan: The feathered mount of the fair goddess Saraswati is said to have a unique gift. It can separate milk from water when the two are mixed. Hence it symbolises the power to distinguish between good and evil, and choose the pure over the impure. This is a quality that wisdom is supposed to bestow on one.

Mouse: There are two accounts that explain why the mouse is the mount of the elephant-headed god. *Yajurveda* writes how Agni, the fire god, was once terrified of Shiva's rage and metamorphosed himself into a mouse to hide

underground. Therefore, the mouse has a fiery quality. Like the flames, it can yield many benefits if it is in harness, but will wreak havoc if it spins out of control. In another account, a curse had transformed a Gandharva (one of a semi-divine race) to a mouse. As it was scampering about in the abode of the sage Parashar, Ganesha threw a dice at it and brought the restless creature in his grip. This gave the god of prosperity the power to rein in fickle-minded Fate. The puny creature also makes a virtue of accumulation and storage, another necessity for commercial success.

Peacock: Kartik's mount is as beautiful as its lord. Yet it stands for control over the six inherent vices in man—

passion, anger, greed, wine, infatuation, vanity and envy. No wonder, the warlord is himself a bachelor.

2

Roster of Rituals

Durga Puja is said to be the festival of kings, so grand and elaborate are the paraphernalia involved. The process is detailed in a number of Puranas.[1] While most other pujas are done in a day or two, Durga Puja takes a minimum of four.[2] The requirements, too, entail that preparations for the Puja begin months in advance. A look at the ingredients for *mahasnan*, the daily bath of the goddess, for instance, reveals how it involves the high and the low, the near and the far, the little and the great, the bitter and the sweet, totalling to almost 75 items![3] Durga is, after all, the goddess of all things and beings.

Topping the list is 18 types of soil—from an ant-hill, a mountain, a temple door, a palace door, a prostitute's door, both sides of a river and a four-cornered crossing, to name a few. The relevance of soil from the prostitute's door may seem to be a questionable inclusion on a holy occasion. But the logic behind the choice is that men leave their virtues behind at the doorstep of a prostitute's chamber, making the spot a potent one. This is also a way to recognise her place in a festival that encompasses all strata of society.

The celebration of power is reflected in prescriptions for soil dug out by a boar with its tooth, by an ox with its horns and by an elephant with its tusk.

The water required is also no less varied—hot, cold, rain water, from the sea, the fountain, the pond, dew collected on lotus pollens, from the Ganga, from the Saraswati (a major North Indian river in Vedic times but now more of a mythical entity) as well as from the various pilgrimages.

Also needed are five jewels, five produces of the cow, extracts of five bitter fruits and a mix of five sweetening ingredients. The water is scented with extracts of fragrant woods and then poured from various containers—pots, pitchers and sprinklers with 1,000 nozzles. There are directives of even the kind of music and the instruments that are to be played during the Devi's bath. For instance, when rainwater is used for the bathing ritual, it has to be Raga Lalit and the trumpet while during a spring water bath, the accompaniment changes to Raga Baradi and the blowing of conch shells.

Of course, it is not the clay image that is bathed. The water is poured on a mirror, capturing the goddess' reflection. It is after this elaborate affair that the puja starts.

Pitritarpan (tribute to the forefather): On Mahalaya, the day before the divine fortnight, the banks of the holy river Ganga are crowded with men immersed in waist-deep water, facing the sun and chanting mantras with hands clasped. It is time to offer water to the forefathers. This is the day of the new moon preceding the divine fortnight. Though during this period, it is night in heaven and the gods are asleep, it is daytime in the nether world and the inhabitants of this region are up and thirsty. On this day,

Hymns on the AIR

Nowhere has Raghunandan[4], the great 16th century Sanskrit scholar, mentioned this in his celebrated methodology of Durga Puja, but Mahalaya today is incomplete without a radio broadcast at dawn. A reading of *Shri Shri Chandi* in the sonorous voice of Birendra Krishna Bhadra, interspersed with devotional songs, wakes people up to the delightful message that the Pujas are here. The programme, which has attained cult status, was first broadcast in 1930, but on a

Sashthi morning. On getting a nod from the then station director of All India Radio, J.R. Stapleton, the team of Premankur Atarthi, Nripendranath Majumdar, Raichand Boral, Pankaj Mullick, Banikumar, Bhadra and others got cracking. At 2 am, the artistes, dressed in traditional Bengali attire, would be picked up from home for what was for the first few years a live broadcast. Later, the audio rights of the programme were sold to the Gramophone Company of India, and the *Mahishasuramardini* album has remained the top grosser every Puja ever since. Such is its popularity that the music company has even brought out a VCD based on the radio programme. Today, the television channels also beam audio-visual versions of the destruction of the buffalo demon, but nothing matches up to the vintage Bhadra and company.

the distance between the terrestrial and the nether world is said to be the least. Pitritarpan may not be directly linked to the Puja, but the Hindu religion places so much importance on duties to the ancestors that such offerings are mandatory for the Puja to take place. Even Rama, the epic hero of the *Ramayana*, had to propitiate his forefathers in the Ikshaku family before invoking Durga.

For all practical purposes, the countdown for the Puja starts from this day.

Bodhan (the awakening), **amantran** (the invitation) and **adhibash** (taking shelter): The evening of Sashthi, Day VI, is when the action begins and the site is the foot of a *bel* tree, said to be a favourite with Lord Shiva. The all-important *ghot*, a pot full of holy water representing the goddess' spiritual presence, is placed there[5]. The tree is imagined as a form of Shiva, described in the mantras as having matted hair and a third eye, clad in tiger skin and riding a bull. The Devi, asleep in the months approaching winter solstice, is then invoked to rise, come down and rest on a branch of the tree and bless the worshipper just as she had blessed Rama, the epic hero. Some 22 items (ranging from sandal paste and pebble to flowers and yoghurt) are needed to complete the next stage in which the Durga idol and the Nabapatrika are also worshipped. It is now permissible to decorate and arm the image. The *bel* tree is then squared off with sticks planted at four corners and tied with red strings. The idea is to keep off the unholy spirits till the day dawns for the worship to begin. It may be pointed out that *bodhan* is as much the awakening of the goddess as of the worshipper's self, making him attain the purity and the consciousness that the task requires. Just as *chakshudan* on Day VII is not just the priest touching the Devi's eyes with a stalk of *bel* leaf dipped in *kajol* (collyrium) and bringing the orbs to 'life', but also opening the inner eye of the worshipper, and gifting him supreme knowledge and realisation.

Bathing of Nabapatrika: This ritual on the morning of Saptami (Day VII) introduces Durga as a goddess of vegetation. A branch is cut off from the *bel* tree at the foot of which the *bodhan* took place the evening before. The branch is where the divine spirit is believed to have descended and rested through the night. It is split into two halves. One half is placed on the representative ghot in front of the image. Branches of eight other trees (banana, paddy, turmeric, etc) are collected and along with the other half of the *bel* branch, they are tied together with a creeper. Durga is present is each of these plants with a distinct name and form.

This collection of nine branches now is taken to the nearest waterbody (or a temple, if a waterbody is not close by) to be bathed. It is quite a procession that meanders down to the riverbank—the priest carrying the Nabapatrika, preceded by the *dhakis* (drummers) and followed by the women of the house or the locality blowing conch shells. After the bath, the Nabapatrika is returned to the site of the puja, wrapped around with a sari and placed on a wooden seat to the right of the goddess. Usually, it is installed to the extreme right of the entourage, making its place adjacent to Ganesha. A vermilion streak is applied to the border of the sari where the forehead would be. Any representation of Durga, a wife, has to carry that mark of a married non-widowed Hindu woman.

This is followed by the great bathing of the goddess, using the mirror on the pot, as described at the beginning of the chapter. The clay idol is now invested with the divine spirit. Separate offerings are made to each god, his or her mount, Mahishasura, the Nabapatrika, Shiva and Vishnu (consorts of Durga and Laxmi) and even the gods painted on the *chalchitra* (see box).

Kaash flowers (catkins), the most familiar herald of the season

Durga as Ganesh-*janani* (mother of Ganesha)

Lotuses being offered to the Goddess, adorned in *sola*-pith decorations

Pitritarpan being done in the Ganga on the morning of Mahalaya

A procession on its way to the river for the bathing of the Nabapatrika
on Saptami morning

Kumari Puja at Belur Math

The glow of lamps announces the beginning of Sandhi Puja

The last ritualistic glimpse of the Goddess in the reflection on Vijaya Dashami

Women queue up for *Deviboron* at a family puja on Vijaya Dashami

Red is the colour of joy as *sindur khela* takes place at a pandal
on Vijaya Dashami

Aarati being offered at a family puja

Dhakis in action

Light of devotion

Prasaad ready for distribution
among devotees

Immersion processions wind their way
to the Ganga

The idol placed on a plank between two boats in the middle of the river,
just before immersion

Gachchha gachchha paramsthanang, swashthaanang parameshwari
Sangbatsare byatite tu punaraagamanaya cha
(Go, go to the supreme place, thy own place, O Heavenly One
And come again a year later)

Pictorial backdrop

The *chalchitra* is an intricately designed hemispherical backdrop to the goddess. Its base is usually blue, the colour of the sky, and the border is densely populated with sketches of a variety of figures from the scriptures. Bringing the unlimited within limits, showing the universal in the particular—that is what the *chalchitra* does, reminding us of the all-pervasiveness of the goddess. The figures include Shiva (at the centre, above Durga), the two other members of the Trinity—Brahma and Vishnu, other forms of Durga, scenes from the Shumba-Nishumba myth, the *Ramayana* or the *Mahabharata*, the great churning of the sea, deeds of Lord Krishna, Shuk-Shari (the mythical pair of birds) and the like. The choice of figures differs from house to house and depends on tradition. Another logic behind the inclusion of other gods is that many divine entities descend on earth on these days to witness Durga Puja. Though they cannot be included in the main frame, their presence is thus acknowledged and they are included in the list of the worshipped. It is also a reminder that Durga evolved out of so many other gods.

Kumari Puja (worship of a virgin): The proceedings on Ashtami (Day VIII) take into account all forms of the goddess. Even her weapons, jewellery and seat are worshipped. This is followed by the worship of a virgin girl. She could be aged one to 16 years and should be unmarried, not embroiled in worldly affairs, not given to outbursts of passion and not into her menstrual cycle. Though a daughter of a Brahmin (the highest caste of priests) is the usual stipulation, the *Devipurana* prescribes a Kshatriya (caste of warriors) girl for a puja seeking a boon of victory, a Vaishya (the trading

Kumari Puja at Belur Math

Belur Math, the headquarters of the Ramakrishna Math and Mission, on the outskirts of Calcutta, holds the most famous Kumari Puja in the country. The Durga Puja here was initiated by Swami Vivekananda in 1901. The resolution to worship the Goddess (*sankalpa*) was taken in the name of Sarada Ma, wife of the great ascetic Ramakrishna Paramhansa. On Ashtami that year, several virgins were worshipped, with Vivekananda himself performing the rites for one of them. The tradition continues to this day. On Day VIII, a girl aged between five and seven is selected and dressed in a red Benarasi sari, ornaments and floral decorations. Earlier the ritual took place in the *natmandir* in front of the image, but the rush of devotees has shifted the venue to the open verandah where the girl is seated on a wooden throne.

community) girl for profits, a Shudra (menials) daughter for the birth of a son, and a female offspring of the Antajas (the untouchables) for deliverance from impending danger.

The goddess has to be worshipped in separate forms depending on the age of the chosen girl. For instance, a two-year-old is conceived of as Saraswati, at 13 she is Mahalaxmi and at 16, Ambika. If the clay image serves to help human beings visualise the goddess, a living entity like the virgin girl further brings the concept within our comprehension.

It is difficult to explain the Devi as a virgin from within the bounds of human experience. But that is what she is, according to the scriptures, so what if she is wife to Lord Shiva. As Kumari, she is neither born of any womb, nor has she borne life in her womb.

In the morning, the chosen girl is bathed in holy water and dressed in a new sari. She is then bedecked with flowers and jewellery. Her feet are washed and the borders are painted with *aalta* (a red dye). A dotted mark of vermilion is put on her forehead. A flower taken from the goddess' hand is given to the girl. She has to fast from the morning till the puja is over. The curling wisps of smoke from the incense sticks, the chanting of the mantras and the beat of the *dhak* lend an other-worldly aura to the girl who is worshipped as a living goddess. When the pujas get over, handsome offerings are to be made—clothings, ornaments and the like.

This ritual is said to multiply manifold the pious rewards of worshipping Durga. In some houses, there is also a tradition of holding Kumari Puja on Day IX instead of Day VIII.

Sandhi Puja (worship at conjunction): This ritual is called such as it takes place at the conjunction of Ashtami, Day VIII, and Nabami, Day IX. More specifically, the period of worship is the last 24 minutes of Day VIII and the first 24 minutes of Day IX. To explain this timing, one has to go back to the Mahishasura myth. During the buffalo-demon's battle with Durga, Chanda and Munda, his two generals, came to attack her with huge reinforcements. At this, the Devi's countenance turned black in anger. From her third eye emerged a frightening female form—bearing a falchion, with a huge face and red eyes, blood dripping from the tongue. This figure let out a tremendous roar and beheaded the two generals with her chopper. The time of that encounter was this period, during which every year Durga is worshipped as Chamunda, the destroyer of Chanda and Munda. The hour is also memorable for the killing of Ravana by Rama, who was blessed and empowered to do so by Durga.

The ingredients that make up the mandatory list for this ritual are 108 lotuses, uncut fruits, sunned rice, 108 lamps, *bel* leaves, hyacinth garlands, clothes and ornaments. More offerings are made according to traditions in individual families. After Sandhi Puja, sacrifices are made to propitiate this ferocious face of the goddess. Though it was customary to kill oxen or goats (even human beings in some rare cases till a century ago) in the Devi's name, in most houses now people make do with the chopping of fruits, like sugarcane, banana and pumpkin. The chopper has to sever the object at one go, as any obstruction in the act is said to beget ill luck. The sacrifice is an outward representation of what the ritual is about—destruction of the animal forces within man.

Bisharjan (Immersion): This is the principal ritual on Dashami, Day X, the last day of festivities. The *dhak* plays a different beat carrying a mournful air. In the morning, an *aarati* is done with a special lamp made of a paste of rice powder. Conch shells are blown and the beat of the *dhak* and the *kanshor-ghonta* reaches a crescendo. At the end of the puja, the *ghot*s, left at the same spot through the three days and touched only by the priest, are moved. The mirror on which the daily bathing of the goddess used to take place is floated in a container full of water. Devotees take a last glimpse of Durga's face and feet through the reflection. Then the priest covers the container.

While the Puja is over at this stage for all symbolic purposes, the clay image is still there to be immersed. Certain customs have been added on to this day through social usage. One such is *sindur khela* (vermilion festival). A preserve of married women, it brings Durga in a sorority, adding to the familial context in which the Devi is worshipped in eastern India. Women apply vermilion to her forehead (the mark of a married woman), caress her face with betel leaf and feed her (touch her lips with) sweets and *paan* (betel leaf). They touch her feet and entreat her to be back the next year. Then wives, young and old, apply vermilion to each other's forehead and bless or seek blessings, as is appropriate for their respective relationships.

In the afternoon, the journey starts for the riverside. The clay images have to be immersed in flowing water. On reaching the bank, the idols are carried bodily to the water, moved around an uneven number of times (three, five or seven times, depending on tradition) and immersed, with the face facing the bank. The stress is on her return the next year. The Nabapatrika, too, is given a watery farewell to the blowing of conch shells and the beat of the *dhak*. Then holy water is sprinkled on one and all as a shower of peace.

Another social custom post-immersion is to return home and write out the Devi's name on a leaf in red ink. A milk-based intoxicant is prepared in some households and passed around, even if in spoonfuls. This is called *siddhi*, which ensures what the name denotes, i.e. attainment of success. Sweets of all shapes and sizes are on offer as people go around touching the feet of elders. Neighbours hug each other as all enmity and acrimony are forgotten. The mood is of celebration—of the victory of good over evil. Hence the name—Vijaya Dashami, the victorious tenth day.

Setting the dates

The dates of the Puja are not fixed and are arrived at every year through calculations by almanac-makers. Most Hindu festivals are determined on the basis of the lunar calendar, or more precisely, the luni-solar calendar, and the movement of the moon is what marks out the fall of the divine fortnight—right after the new moon on Mahalaya.

Planetary conjunctions on the days of arrival (Day VII) and departure (Day X of the divine fortnight) of the Devi are

Down the almanac lane

There are two schools of thought among the almanac makers—Surya Siddhanta and Visuddha Siddhanta. Surya Siddhanta is an older method of computation laid down in around 400 AD. In early 16th century, Raghunandan, the great scholar, prepared the format followed in modern almanacs. But over the centuries, it was found that the calculated positions of the heavenly bodies, as published, did not agree with their actual positions in the sky. The reason was the cumulative angular shift of the stars had not been taken into account. This was particularly noticeable during the eclipses. This lead to the birth of Visuddha Siddhanta, based on positional astronomical data. To put an end to the controversy, the Union government formed the calendar reform committee, under physicist Dr Meghnad Saha, in 1953, which upheld the Visuddha Siddhanta. Yet the Surya Siddhanta almanacs have retained their popularity, selling more than a lakh at home and abroad, in books and CD ROMs.

are also said to decide how it augurs for the rest of the year. The key is the mode of transport that the goddess is supposed to take on her way here or back. The daughter of the Himalayas has all the travel options that used to be available in the land of the Himalayas in the days when her puja started with fanfare—the boat, the elephant, the horse and the palanquin.

The boat: If the boats are in use, the rivers have to be full to the brim. This, in turn, presupposes a good monsoon and therefore a good harvest. *Noukayang shasyabriddhistathaajalam*

The elephant: The steady and stately stride of the elephant reaps an earth full of crops. *Gaje cha jalada debi shashyapurna vasundhara*

The horse: Scattering the soil, raising dust and causing a ruckus with the clutter of the hooves, a journey on the horse ushers in devastation. The dry soil is the alarm signal for a drought. *Ghotake chhatrabhangasturongome*

The palanquin: The swinging of the palanquin breeds uncertain times. A famine is in order. *Dolaayaang marakang bhabet*

There is a *sloka* which serves as a formula to link the day of the week on which the Puja proper starts or ends and the Devi's chosen mode of transport that year.

Rabou chondre gajarurha ghotake shani bhoumayoh,
Gurou Shukrey cha dolayang noukayang budhabasharey

On Sunday and Monday, she rides an elephant; on Saturday, it's a horse that carries her; she travels in a palanquin on Thursday and Friday; Wednesday is the day for a voyage in a boat. Though the two schools of thought among the almanac-makers—Surya Siddhanta and Visuddha

Siddhanta—sometimes differ by a few minutes or hours in calculations of puja timings[6], both follow the *sloka* in deducing the fateful mode of travel from the days on which the Puja falls.

An elephant-elephant combination is the best as that guarantees a good year both before and after the puja. The worst case scenario, correspondingly, is arrival by horse and departure by the palanquin or vice versa. If the two journeys have to be on opposite notes, people hope for the departure to be a positive indicator so that there are favourable times to look forward to after the Pujas. But as this is based on astrological calculations, devotees do not have any choice in the matter and one can only worship the Devi and hope for the best.

3

_____

Of Palaces and Courtyards

When did Durga Puja start? Raja Surath and Rama, who worshipped the deity in spring and autumn respectively, are both mythical figures. To what extent their puja resembles what we see today is also a matter of conjecture.

Though archaelogical evidence of Durga's existence dates back much earlier, Durga Puja, in its present form, is said to have started in the Mughal era in the 16th century. Raja Udaynarayan took the initiative to hold the first puja in around 1580. His dream was a show of strength on the lines of the elaborate Rajasuya[1] or Ashwamedha[2] Yagna that kings organised in mythical times.

But most historians conclude that Udaynarayan could not fulfil his dream. It was left to his grandson Raja Kangshanarayan to achieve the feat. Kangshanarayan created a stir in his time by organising Durga Puja at an expense of about Rs 8 lakh at Taherpur in the Rajshahi district of undivided Bengal (now in Bangladesh).[3]

Unanimity, however, exists about a puja that took place a little later—in 1606. The worshipper was Bhabananda Majumdar of Nadia, ancestor of Raja Krishna Chandra Roy. In 1610, another puja—perhaps the first in Calcutta—was launched by Laxmikanta Majumdar, founder of the Sabarna Roy Chowdhury family. The zamindar family is linked to the history of Calcutta for the sale of land rights to the East India Company of three villages that formed the city decades later. Both Bhabananda and Laxmikanta came to prominence thanks to the titles and largesse bestowed on them for services rendered to the empire by Raja Man Singh, general of Emperor Akbar and later, ruler of Amber.

Other Hindu kings came forward as well and the Puja spread far and wide to Gaur, Rajmahal, Murshidabad and Krishnanagar. Soon, Durga Puja became the most important annual festival, offering the local landed gentry the chance to flex their financial muscle and also bringing together family, friends and neighbours, infusing life in the placid rural community.

Festive fervour in the villages centred around the puja in the house of the raja or the local zamindar. Large-scale feasts and gifts of clothes and foodgrains on these days added to the cheer. Everyone had a slice of the action. Some offered to fetch water from the Ganges, some were assigned the job of finding 'faultless' animals for sacrifice, others washed the puja utensils or collected flowers and *bel* leaves. It was a busy time for the professional communities too. The potter would be up at night giving shape to the pots and urns, the sprinkler for the Devi's baths, 108 lamps for Sandhi puja and the like. The artisan got busy with the idol. The priest shifted address to the palace even before the start of the festival. The cobbler or the blacksmith did duty as *dhaki*; the milkman's wife coated the puja courtyard with cowdung and clay. The barber's wife came over to adorn the feet of the women of the house with *aalta*. The weaver readied stocks to supply all family members with new clothes. People, who stayed away on work the rest of the year, would be back home during this period. And when it was time for the Devi's *bodhan*, the entire village flocked at the courtyard of the zamindar's house.

Glory in the glitter

There are numerous accounts of splendour in such festivals. Raja Krishna Chandra Roy (1710-1782), ruler of Nadia, organised one of the most lavish pujas of his time. In his palace in Krishnanagar, work on the clay idol started on the holy day of the Ultarath festival (the day of the return journey of Lord Jagannath in his chariot) in the month of Asharha (June-July) with the firing of a cannon. Durga was dressed as a warrior, clad in armour and masculine apparel. Her mount was not a lion but a mythical creature: half-man, half-lion. The number 108 played a key role in all rituals. The volume of clay used for creating the images was 108 maunds. The morning of Saptami would announce the start of the puja to the flourish of the beat of 108 *dhak*s. The lotuses used in the puja numbered 108. As many as 108 goats were sacrificed. And during immersion, 108 carriers transported the goddess from the palace to the Jalangi river about two miles away. The influence of the nawabs of Murshidabad (rulers of the province of Bengal, appointed by Mughal decree who were virtually independent before the British replaced them) had rubbed off on Krishna Chandra. He introduced nautches to add to the festive cheer.[4]

The October 17, 1829, edition of *Samachar Darpan*[5] points to the ruler from Krishnanagar as the one to have transformed the festival into a glitzy affair. "It is due to this (the Raja's puja) that the rich are no longer afraid to flaunt their wealth before the British rulers and are increasingly spending more (author's translation)," the chronicle wrote.

Krishna Chandra, credited with starting many of the modern practices of worship, also did much for the spread of Durga Puja. He issued orders to the zamindars under him to start the autumnal festival and even offered financial help to those who could not afford it.

Another illustrious worshipper was Gobindaram Mitra (1720-1756), the 'black zamindar'[6] appointed by the East India Company, who used to hold the pujas in his ancestral home in Kumortuli, in north Calcutta. The Mitra family documents describe how the goddess had a silver throne to herself and her sons. Shiva was included in the entourage, and towered over the rest. The Laxmi and Saraswati figures were placed at the sides and during immersion carried in separate decorated palanquins. Preparations for the festivities started about a fortnight in advance. Large-scale charity, feasts and musical soirees were the order of the days. Yet the merriment did not lighten the depth of devotion.

There was a saying in those days that the Devi did three things during her stay—deck herself up in jewellery, have a hearty meal and enjoy the entertainment. Though every family put its grandest foot forward for the festival, public opinion decided on a definite address for each of these activities, thereby crowning these pujas in the eyes of the contemporary and posterity.

It was at Shib Krishna Dawn's Jorasanko residence that Durga was said to put on her jewellery. And why not? Dawn, a coal and iron merchant, covered his idol in gold. Through the four days, Durga was present in all her glittering glory at the Dawn home. It was said in those days that the ornaments of diamonds and emeralds were specially ordered from Paris.[7]

She partook of the meals at the Kumortuli address of Abhaycharan Mitra, great grandson of Gobindaram. It is fascinating to read accounts of the spread laid out at the puja, especially the sweets. Contemporary actor and dramatist Amritalal Basu remembers how the *jalebi*s were as big as cartwheels, the *gajaa*s were like huge circular plates and the *motichur*s rivalled cannon balls in size. The sweets piled up, touching the ceiling of the hall.[8]

As for the entertainment, her seat was booked at the palatial mansion of the Debs in Sovabazar. Nautches by the finest bayaderes in the country started late in the evening and continued well into the night, punctuated by music, mimicry and masquerade. More on that revelry later.

Any account of Durga Puja in the 19th century remains incomplete without anecdotes about intoxicated organisers. One is mentioned in *Hutom Pnyachar Naksha*, the great social chronicle of mid-19th century Bengal. Inspecting the idol on the night of Sashthi (Day 6), the head of the Singha family, under the influence of liquor, suddenly flew into a rage. "What is that beast doing under the goddess' feet when I, the real lion, am here," he exclaimed. The next moment he had dislodged the clay lion and wrapping himself in a blanket, positioned himself in its place. In the morning, when the priest found him there, his embarrassment can be well-imagined.

Another babu, in his intoxication, took the saying "*dhaki suddho bisharjan*" (immersion along with the drummer) literally. On Dashami (Day X), two boats were rented. One carried the babu and his mates, the other the *dhaki*s. The idol was placed on a plank in between. Once the boat reached mid-Ganga, the boats separated, and the idol was immersed. The beat of *dhak* reached a crescendo. Suddenly the babu's eyes fell on the *dhakis* in the other boat. "Why are you still afloat? The Goddess has set off for Mt Kailash. Don't you know you have to guide her?" he roared. To humour the babu, his flatterers sunk the other boat and the poor *dhakis* had to swim ashore.

The Company connection

The arrival of the British, who, in course of time, got deeply entangled in the country's social fabric, brought about a transformation in the character of the Puja. Contact with the East India Company, commercial or otherwise, led to the emergence of a new moneyed class in Calcutta. By mid-18th century, the greatest festival of the Bengalis had become the occasion for these nouveaux riches babus to flaunt their wealth and further their good offices with the Company representatives. The change is best brought out in an account of J.Z. Holwell, the erstwhile zemindar[9] of Calcutta. In *Important Historical Events*, 1766, he writes: "Doorga Pujah...is the grand general feast of the Gentoos, usually visited by Europeans (by invitation) who are treated by the proprietor of the feast with fruits and flowers in season, and are entertained every evening while the feast lasts, with bands of singers and dancers."[10] A great religious ceremony was thus reduced to a "general feast".

The participation of the Company sahibs was a matter of great prestige for the host. The complacence is unmistakable in a letter Nabakrishna Deb (of Sovabazar lineage), the *talukdar* of north Calcutta, wrote to a friend, announcing Lord Clive's consent to "grace" his Puja.

Nabakrishna, awarded the Raja title by the British, in fact, started his puja to celebrate the East India Company's victory in the Battle of Plassey over Nawab Siraj-ud-Daulah in 1757. A *thakurdalan* (a hall for worship) came up at his palatial Sovabazar residence for the express purpose of hosting the festival. Lord Clive himself is said to have made offerings of baskets of fruits, Rs 101 and even a goat for sacrifice.

The whole of Calcutta, it is said, thronged Nabakrishna's palace. Right after *bodhan*, food and clothes would be distributed among the poor, a practice that continued through the puja days. Around 1,001 animals were sacrificed in course of the festival. A cannon volley announced the beginning of Sandhi Puja, which was both signal and sanction for other households in the locality to start the ritual in their respective pujas. The same practice was followed for the immersion procession as well.

But what took centrestage was the feasting, the dancing and various other forms of entertainment. Missionary William Carey describes a Puja programme at Nabakrishna's residence. "The majority of company crowded to Raja Nabkessen's where several mimics attempted to imitate the manners of different nations."[11]

Not to be outdone by Nabakrishna, a number of other well-off babus started Durga Puja at their residences, which was attended by the British. They included Prankrishna Singha, Keshtochandra Mitra, Narayan Mitra, Ramhari Thakur, Baranashi Ghosh and Darpanarayan Thakur. On September 25, the *Calcutta Chronicle* reported a post-Puja soiree at Sukhmoy Roy's place. "The only novelty that rendered the entertainment different from last year was the introduction, or rather the attempt to introduce some English tunes among the Hindoostanee music..."[12] After Nabakrishna died in 1797, his sons Gopimohan[13] and Rajkrishna carried on with the Sovabazar puja with equal pomp.

The entertainment provided on such occasions to amuse the sahibs became the chief incentive for hosting *Durgotsab*. These "attractions" would also be publicised through advertisements in English newspapers.

This is what Prankrishna Haldar of Chinsurah brought out in the *Calcutta Gazette* on September 20, 1817.

Grand Nautches on Doorga Pooja Holidays:

Baboo Prankrishna Holdar of Chinsurah:

Begs to inform the Ladies and Gentlemen, and the Public in General that he has commenced giving a Grand Nautch from this day, that it will continue till the 29th Inst. Those Ladies and Gentlemen who have received Invitation tickets, are respectfully solicited to favour him with their Company on the days mentioned above; and those to whom the Invitation Tickets have not been sent (strangers to the Baboo), are also respectfully solicited to favour him with their Company.

Baboo Prankissen Holdar further begs to say, that every attention and respect will be paid to the Ladies and Gentlemen who will favour him with their Company, and that he will be happy to furnish them with Tifin [sic], Diner [sic], Wines &c., during their stay there.[14]

The journals in those days gave extensive coverage to the amusements, with special reference to the attendance of the British guests. *The Bengal Hurkaru* on 12 October, 1829, reports on that year's puja at Sovabazar: "At about ten o'clock Rajas Shibkrishen and Kalikrishen with their brothers had the great honour of receiving Lord Cambermere suit shortly after which came in Lord and Lady Bentinck with their suites, when 'God save the King' was struck up, and their Lordships were seated on a golden sofa, placed at the centre of the 'nautch' place...The nautches...greatly pleased their Lordships and her Ladyship."[15]

These "nautches" brought to town the best-known names among the bayaderes. A correspondent writes in *Asiatic Journal* in 1816: "...the chief singers Nik-hee and Ashroon, who are engaged by Neel Munee Mullik and Raja Ram Chunder, are still without rivals in melody and grace. A woman named Zeenut, who belongs to Benaras, performs at the house of Budr Nath Baboo in Jora Sanko. Report speaks highly of a young damsel, named Fyz Boksh who performs at the house of Goroo Persad Bhos."[16]

Rajkrishna created a flutter in social circles, organising three consecutive nights of dances. An anonymous Englishman, who was his guest in 1814, is all praise for Nikee, then just into her teens. "I must confess that the twelve hundred rupees (one hundred and fifty pounds), and two pair [sic] of shawls of the same value, the price of Neekhee's attendance for three nights, was only commensurate with her singular accomplishments," he writes in his memoir *Sketches of India*.[17]

The British, as is evident, participated enthusiastically in such festivities. They had *prasaad* and did *pranaam*, often lying prostrate on the ground. The soldiers would salute "Goddess Doorgah". Company auditor-general John Chips even used to organise Durga Puja at his office in Surul, in Birbhum district.[18]

An idea of the Britishers' impressions of the puja can be obtained from accounts left behind by diarists. Their observations on the customs were mostly unalloyed by explanations from locals.

Maria Graham, who published her *Journal of a Residence in India* in 1812, saw "moving temples" being "carried upon men's heads" on October 25, 1810. The divinities, carried in procession with "musical instruments, banners and bare-headed Brahmins repeating muntras (forms of prayer)", were being taken to be "bathed in the Hooghly, which being a branch of the Ganges, is sacred". "The gods were followed by cars, drawn by oxen or horses, gaily caparisoned, bearing the sacrificial utensils, accompanied by other Brahmins, and the procession was closed by an innumerable multitude of people of all castes." Ms Graham also received a printed card on the occasion from the Sovabazar address, which she has transcribed. "Maha Rajah, Raj kissen Bahadur, presents his respectful compliments to Mrs Gram [sic], and requests the honour of his company to a nautch (being Doorga Poojah) ... at nine o'clock in the evening."

If the baboos vied with each other in drawing the big names to their respective pujas, the foreigners too looked forward to receiving the invitations. So Ms Graham "having never seen a nautch", "did not decline the Maha Rajah's invitation" and reached the "fine house at the end of Chitpore bazar" on the appointed evening. The welcome was elaborate: "The host ... led us to the most commodious seat, stationed boys behind us with round fans of red silk, with gold fringe, and then presented us with bouquets of the mogree and the rose, tied up in a green leaf, ornamented with silver fringe. A small gold vase being brought, the Maha Rajah, with a golden spoon, perfumed us with ottur, and sprinkled us with rose-water, after which we were allowed to sit still and look on."

The entertainment on all three evenings was spectacular and Ms Graham took in every detail of the nautch. "The first dancers were men, whom by their dress, I took for women, though... These gave way to some Cashmerian singers, whose voices were very pleasing. ... I was sorry when they finished, to make way for a kind of pantomime in which men impersonated elephants, bears and monkeys. ...The best amusement we staid [sic] to partake of was the exhibition of a ventriloquist (the best I ever heard)." She also mentions "a masquerade, when several Portuguese and Pariahs appeared as Europeans, and imitated our dances, music and manners".[19]

But not everyone trusted their own judgment and depended on explanations from "natives". Maria, Lady Nugent, wife of the then commander-in-chief in India Sir George Nugent, stayed in the country from 1811 to 1815. Her counsellor seems to have been her ayah who must have had her tongue firmly in cheek while explaining the nuances of the rituals. An entry in Lady Nugent's diary, dated Friday, October 1, 1812, describes "Doorgah" thus: "She is represented by a figure made of painted mud, with large silver eyes, which a Brahmin, concealed behind her, opens and shuts continually. ...A plantain tree is placed before her, for her eyes to rest upon; the effects of these silver orbs being supposed to be fatal to any human being; and my ayah assured me, whatever she put her eye upon would instantly die..."[20]

The backlash and the decline

As wine and beef from Wilson's Hotel became the toast of the nights of revelry, and entertainment took on cruder avatars with every passing autumn, resentment at the hedonistic perversions in the name of Durga Puja started building up in many quarters. Sarcasm at the state of affairs is dripping from a piece by Bhabanicharan Bandyopadhyay in 1823, entitled *Kolikata Kamalalay*: "Durga Puja in Calcutta is better described as a festival of chandeliers, lamps, poets, nautch girls, or even of the wife's ornaments and clothes. (author's translation)"[21] The *Calcutta John Bull* of October

13, 1819, agrees: "The nautches, it must be confessed, have of late, acquired rather a bad name."[22] Sir Radhakanta Deb, son of Nabakrishna's nephew and foster son Gopimohan, is said to have incurred the wrath of the other Hindu gentry for inviting non-believing sahibs at his Puja feasts. Questions of racial propriety began to be raised. People were also becoming conscious of their rights and liberties and were no longer afraid to hold their own on the religious front, keeping the British at arm's length.

One act of defiance that became part of contemporary lore was that of Rani Rashmoni's. The widow of Rajchandra Das carried on with the puja started by her father-in-law with increased splendour at her Jaanbazar address in north Calcutta. One year, a European gentleman complained about the din during the Nabapatrika procession to the river. She retaliated by bringing out an even noisier procession the next day. A case was filed and she was fined Rs 50. The rani paid the fine but blocked the road to thoroughfare, pointing out that it was built by her husband. The British were forced to negotiate with her and return the fined amount.

Intra-family strifes in the houses of the noble also took their toll on the pujas. An analysis of the trend in *Bengal Spectator* puts the finger on "loss of money by litigation and other causes of an adventurous nature", and the fact that "The junior members of some of the native families are no friends of Heathenism…".[23]

The *Samachar Darpan* reflects in 1829 how the song and dance routine used to be "five times grander in the immediate past". "The festivities are on the wane, without doubt (author's translation)," it concluded.[24]

And with the promulgation of a law in 1840 prohibiting Company officials from attending native social occasions, the interest of the babus in hosting Durga Puja waned.

4

From Courtyards to Street Corners

If individual initiative for Durga Puja was on the decline, collective enterprise came to replace it.

The pujas in the house of the raja or the zamindar provided ample avenues of participation for the common people. As his subjects, they could also claim some relationship with the organiser, and by extension, his puja. Yet hierarchy was strictly maintained and all decisions about the puja were imposed from the top.

What the rich and famous started off in their houses was an imitation of these aristocratic religious occasions that sought to retain the same grandeur in outward show, albeit for the sake of social prestige. But there was hardly a link to the common people in these cases unlike the ties that bound the raja or the zamindar to his tenants. The *Asiatic Journal* writes in 1816 how during the Devi's stay "the houses of the wealthier Bengalees are thrown open for the reception of every class of the inhabitants of this great city"[1]. But there was no guarantee of intimate participation for local residents, nor any certainty of permission for their entry. At Sovabazar, the entertainment was free for all for 12 days, starting from the ninth day of the preceding cycle of the waning moon when *bodhon* of the Deb family puja took place. But on the three big nights, when the British were invited over, entry was severely restricted. Insults and abuses were not unknown either. Dramatist Amritalal Basu recalls: "For the British, there was some sherry, champagne, brandy, biscuit (at the Deb's); a few lucky Bengalis were also allowed a share. But at mealtime, Bengalis were a strict no-no and those uninvited were booted out (author's translation)."[2] The common man never had much of a say in the pujas and now his space was shrinking. It is in this context that the concept of community puja germinated.

The start came from the districts. Around 1790, twelve Brahmin friends in Guptipara, about 80 km from Calcutta in the Hooghly district, decided to institute a puja on their own after being denied entry at a household ritual.[3] A journal, *The Friend of India*, writes in May, 1820: "...a new species of Pooja has been introduced into Bengal within the last thirty years, called Barowaree... About thirty years ago, at Goopti-para, near Santipoora... a number of Brahmins formed an association for the celebration of a Pooja independently... They elected twelve men as a Committee from which circumstance it takes its name, and solicited subscriptions in all the surrounding villages."[4]

This was a bold step, as the pujas so far had been the preserve of the mighty and the moneyed. Subscriptions were raised from neighbours and the Devi was worshipped, if not with pomp and pageantry then with diligence of devotion. The kings in myths or in history might have sought boons of greater splendour or success in war, but for the common people, the greatest catalyst for invoking the goddess was fear of famine. According to *Hutom Pnayachar Naksha*, "The custom of twelve or more people coming together to worship Kali or any other god was instituted during an epidemic (author's translation)."[5]

Thus started the *baro-yaar-i* (of twelve friends) or *baroari* puja in Bengal. It gained popularity in leaps and bounds. Here at last was a concept that brought the Devi among the masses to be worshipped by them as their means permitted. Thus Durga Puja went democratic years before the country did.

Collections for the first *baroari* puja reached a figure of almost Rs 7,000. As the community puja travelled from Guptipara to neighbouring towns like Santipur, Kanchrapara and Chinsurah, it became more ambitious. *Hutom Pnyachar Naksha* mentions that the Santipur puja was well-known for its princely budget and gigantic images. Entertainment was the big draw at Chinsurah, with even *babus* from Calcutta voyaging down in their personal boats to watch clowns in action, contests among poets and such typical amusements of local folk culture.

Collection overdrive

Since collection of subscriptions from one and all was the defining point and sole source of revenue for the *baroari* puja, the organisers took the business seriously. By 1840, the practice had become such a menace to local residents that the magistrate of 24-Parganas, Mr Patton, had to travel incognito in a palanquin to put an end to the subscription drive launched in the area by the boys of Behala. That the collection had reached the extent of extortion is clear from the report on February 27, 1840, in *The Calcutta Courier* on Mr Patton's initiative:

> In consequence of the oppressive extortions of money by some young men belonging to the family of the Saborno Chowdries of Bihala of Zilla 24-Parganas, under the pretext of meeting the expense of a Barrowarry Poojah, it was impossible for anybody, especially females, to pass that road in a conveyance without satisfying their unjust and illegal demands. When they happened to see a woman coming in a palanqeen [sic], they immediately stopped it and if a handsome present was not offered, a volley of abuse was heaped on the poor creature. As women, from a sense of decency and decorum, were unable to resist these demands, they were sometimes compelled to give their clothes and ornaments when they had no money about them.[6]

The fact that a *baroaritala* (a community space to host the pujas) existed in Behala proves that the concept had reached Calcutta by then, though it took a long time to take shape. But it is doubtful whether the Saborno Chowdhury family was directly involved in raising subscriptions, as the zamindars must have been affluent enough to have organised their puja with their own resources.

Soon after, Shib Krishna Dawn took the initiative in collecting subscriptions from fellow traders. In those days, it was mainly the trading community that was involved in holding *baroari* pujas. Money-lenders and shop-keepers would contribute round the year at a fixed rate proportionate to their volume of business. Once that collection reached a sizeable amount, it was kept in the custody of one of the respected and better-off traders who was named the committee secretary. It was his responsibility to collect subscriptions and arrange for the entertainment during the pujas.[7]

Subscription drives gave rise to incidents both cruel and humorous. A reader, in a letter to the editor published in *Somprakash*, on June 23, 1862, writes how Durga Puja was being held ceremoniously in a village in Tribeni where people were dying, being unable to afford medicines. Those who had refused to pay had their utensils taken away.[8]

Collectors used novel methods to rein in those unwilling to contribute. Several incidents are documented in *Hutom Pnyachar Naksha*.

There was a one-eyed merchant in the city who was known for being stingy. When subscriptions were sought from him, he refused, saying it was not his habit to waste his hard-earned money. He challenged the collectors to point out a single instance of unnecessary expenditure in his house. The hapless collectors looked around. Children's clothes, pillow covers—everything had been tailored by the babu himself. When his *dhoti*s wore out he exchanged the rags for utensils. Neither did he spend a single pie from the interests accruing from his share certificates.

Suddenly it struck them that the one-eyed man's spectacles had two lenses. "Sir, either you contribute or you remove a lens," they said. Thus cornered, the merchant reluctantly parted with two 25-paisa coins. In another incident, fund-collectors gheraoed one Singha babu[9], yelling "Got him, got him." They explained that Goddess Durga had appeared in their dreams and informed them that she was stuck on her way from the Himalayas as her mount, the lion, had broken a leg. She needed a *singha* (lion) to complete the journey. Pleased at their witticism, Singha babu contributed handsomely.

In the initial years, collecting subscriptions was a tough task. With weeks to go before the Pujas, the organisers would start knocking at doors, employing every trick—from persuasion to threats. There were no printed receipt books. The group would be carrying a wooden box or cloth bags in which the cash was collected. In special cases, subscription was collected in kind—fruits, vegetables and the like. Even then, at some doors, taunts from the gate-keeper were all that they could gather.

Some organisers did not react well to refusals. A common way of punishing a stubborn householder was leaving a Durga idol in his house on the sly so that he was forced to hold a puja, and spend many times the amount the organisers would have been happy with. *Samachar Darpan,* on October 13, 1832, mentions how this mischievous practice was becoming a growing menace. But some householders were plucky enough to disregard social criticism and overcome pious meekness. In an incident which took place in suburban Belghoria in 1820, a man was so infuriated on seeing an idol left in his courtyard that he ordered it to be dismembered and immersed in the river (*Samachar Darpan*, September 23, 1820).[10]

Rivalry between neighbouring localities too was intense. Once Santipur spent Rs 5 lakh for Durga Puja, preparations for which had gone on for seven years. So huge was the idol that it had to be dismembered for immersion. This prompted the organisers in neighbouring Guptipara to hold a puja where Ganesha was in unbleached cloth, mourning his mother's "death" (at the hands of their rivals from Santipur) in accordance with Bengali Hindu custom.[11]

The community avatar in Calcutta

"*Sarbojanin Durgotsab*" (everyone's Durga festival), as we know it today, started much later in Calcutta. This takes the concept to an all-inclusive form, more expansive than the strictly local *baroari*. The year 1910 saw a puja organised in Bhowanipur, on Sanatan Basu Ghat Road (in south Calcutta). The organiser was Sanatan Dharmotsahini Sabha. Though the word was not used, it was *sarbojanin* in spirit. Around the same time, similar festivals started in Ramdhan Mitra Lane and Sikdar Bagan. Then came Simla Byayam Samiti and Bagbazar Sarbojanin (started in 1919 as Nebubagan Baroari) in north Calcutta.

Kumortuli Sarbojanin, which started in 1933, deserves special mention for introducing stylistic changes in modelling in 1935. It is perhaps fitting that such changes were scripted in the backyard of Bengal's best-known hub of image-makers.

After holding the puja for two years, the organisers came to Kumortuli's most famous son, Gopeshwar Pal, with requests to supervise the making of the goddess. Gopeshwar had then returned after completing a sculpture course in Italy. He decided to do away with the *ekchala* (single-frame) image and separate the quintet. Nor would he have the figures standing still. He wanted to capture the action involved in the Mahishasura myth. So he designed a battle-hungry Durga, her trident raised to pierce the demon, as it was chased by the lion. Faced with such an unheard-of scheme, Jagadish Pal, the sculptor, quit, feigning illness. So Gopeshwar modelled the image himself. Mahishasura now had rippling muscles to accentuate the glory of Durga's victory over him. The pundits were furious at the break with tradition and the priests initially refused to worship the image.[12] Yet this found favour with people and the style caught on.

Freedom cry

During this time, the freedom movement had reached its peak and Calcutta, in common with the rest of Bengal, was buzzing with terrorist plots and nationalist protests. The biggest contemporary religious event too was sucked into patriotic programmes and used as a front for the meeting and training of freedom-fighters.

The *birashtami* ritual, performed on Ashtami, was the perfect occasion for such activities. From the morning, young men would involve themselves in rigorous contests of stick play, dagger work, martial arts, wrestling and boxing, under the very eyes of the British, but under the guise of religious rites.

The Simla Byayam Samiti puja was started in 1926 and dedicated to the freedom movement by the founder of the Samiti, Atindranath Basu. The names involved with the puja— Saratchandra Basu, Bhupendranath Dutta (Swami Vivekananda's brother), Upendranath Bandyopadhyay, Kiron Mukherjee—belong to front-ranking freedom-fighters. The Samiti held pageants showcasing key chapters of the freedom struggle like the Battle of Plassey and the uprising of 1857. Exhortations to rise and rebel written on red cotton fabric dotted the puja premises.[13] The 1939 edition of the festival was inaugurated by Netaji Subhas Chandra Bose, who was then also the president of the Indian National Congress. Nitai Pal's image that year was special—Durga towering at 21 feet and the hitherto *ekchala* image separated into five frames.[14]

Netaji was also involved with a number of pujas like Kumortuli Sarbojanin and Bagbazar Sarbojanin (being the secretary of both in 1938 and 1939). The Bagbazar puja was known for its elaborate *birashtami* celebration. During the Non-Cooperation movement against the British, arrests became widespread and the Simla Byayam Samiti puja was suspended from 1932 to 1935.

Pandals around Bengal were brimming with patriotic fervour, so much so that Durga herself took on a new avatar—

Bharatmata (Mother India). Novelist Bankimchandra Chattopadhyay, who gave the nation its battle cry *Vande Mataram*, had already depicted this incarnation of the goddess in the nineteenth century, giving the religion of patriotism a deity to invoke and worship, irrespective of the devotee's caste or creed. The mood is best brought out in his novel *Ananda Math*, where the three faces of the Mother Goddess reflect the nation's golden past, its dark and dominated present and a glorious future towards which his countrymen will have to work. A similar, semi-mystic vision is conveyed in one of the sections of his series *Kamalakanta*, called *Amar Durgotsab* (My Durga Festival).

The description struck a resonant chord in every community. Here at last was a unifying icon. Netaji Subhas Chandra Bose used the image in his parting message to his countrymen dated March 2, 1933, before leaving the country: "One of the dreams that have inspired me...is that of a great and undivided Bengal devoted to the service of India and humanity—a Bengal that is ...the home alike of the Moslem, the Hindu, the Christian and the Buddhist. It is this Bengal ... that I worship." The title of the address was "Vision of 'Bharatmata' As She Is Destined To Be".[15]

The vision also inspired organisers of pujas. The writer, Sunil Ganguly, recalls a puja in his childhood in Faridpur (now in Bangladesh). Netaji, who had been put under house arrest by the British, had escaped to Europe in 1941, and people believed him to be the messiah who would come back to free the country from the shackles of the Raj. Ganguly's uncles, then in college, were among those who were keeping faith. The artisan that year was given special instructions about the idol and the image was crafted in secret. On Panchami (Day V), when the veil of secrecy was lifted, the crowd let out a gasp of disbelief. At Durga's feet lay a sahib in military gear—khaki uniform, spiked boots, rifle slung over the shoulder. The Devi, flashing fury from her three eyes, had clutched a tuft of auburn hair. Her mount, the rampant lion, was tearing at his abdomen. Close by, in place of Kartik and Ganesh, stood Subhas Chandra Bose, in *dhoti-punjabi* and *khaddar* cap, an unsheathed sword in his hand.

The word spread, and the *atchala* (eight-pillared hall without walls) was soon brimming with villagers from afar. In place of the customary "Durga *ma ki jai*" (Victory to Goddess Durga), a spontaneous chorus arose in Subhas Bose's name. But this puja, remembers Ganguly, was short-lived. Three days later, on Ashtami, two big boats full of policemen docked at the village ghat. Though the inspector was a Bengali Hindu, he had come as a representative of the British government. The organisers faced threats and reprimands for this "anti-government prank". The Second World War was then raging and the penalty for opposing the government in those times was imprisonment without trial. Ganguly fails to recall if any arrests were made but the puja was stopped, the image was seized and the village had to make do with worshipping just the symbolic *ghot*.[16]

The Bharatmata association took Durga Puja right into prisons sheltering freedom-fighters of Bengal. The Rajshahi Jail (now in Bangladesh) hosted the Devi for some years at the initiative of the inmates. Bhupendranath Dutta writes of an autumn around 1915-16. It was argued that the government had no right to interfere with the religious freedom of prisoners jailed without trial. The chief secretary to the Bengal government, Sir Hugh Stephenson, granted permission to host the puja in association with the jail staffers and sanctioned an amount. A pandal was set up right outside the prison gate. Many dignitaries of the city, including the jail superintendent, paid a visit to the puja. By arrangement with the jailor, the state prisoners were allowed to go out and receive guests. On Ashtami, the patriots treated about 1,200 fellow inmates to *luchi* and sweets. Jogeshchandra Chattopadhyay recalls how at the same jail, in 1918, a white goat was sacrificed to the Devi. The significance of the sacrifice lay in the colour of the goat skin, as the British were largely referred to as "Whites".

The newspaper *Forward* mentions how Netaji managed to wrest permission from the government to hold Durga Puja after a hunger-strike at Mandalay Jail in Burma. At Hijli Jail, women patriots in the freedom movement like Santi Das, Banalata Dasgupta, Indusudha Ghosh and Bina Das also invoked the Mother. Rabindranath Tagore's drama, *Tapati*, was staged to celebrate the occasion. A unique puja was organised in 1906 by Anushilan Samiti, an organisation committed to militant nationalism, at its office at 39, Cornwallis Street in north Calcutta. In place of clay images, there was a cache of arms—spears, swords, daggers, falchions and sticks. The priest was brought over from Maharashtra and eminent names on the British "wanted" list, such as Sri Aurobindo, Bagha Jatin and Jatindramohan Thakur, attended the puja.[17]

When the country achieved Independence in 1947, jubilation swept the puja pandals as well—patriotic songs were played on loudspeakers, portraits of freedom-fighters lined the pandal walls... The Devi could now openly be worshipped as Bharatmata, proud Tricolour in hand. Writer Kabita Sinha recalls how in one puja, organised by women, Aparna Debi, daughter of freedom-fighter Chittaranjan Das, sang *Vande Mataram* at the cultural programmes organised every evening. A guessing game was held with a participation fee pegged at 10 paise. The proceeds went to buy bedding materials and clothes for the revolutionary, Ullaskar Dutta, who had just returned as a penniless man from the Andaman Islands where he had been serving a life term.[18]

Puja in times of peril

Durga Puja has always been associated with service to society. During the Great Famine of 1943 the festivities were completely wiped out by the dance of death and devastation that overtook Bengal. With the food-grain crisis at its peak, the hungry hordes crying on the streets and entire families succumbing to starvation, it was unseemly to indulge in entertainment. Organisers of most pujas shunned excesses and took to serving the unfed. No communal distinction was made as Hindus and Muslims queued up together for *prasad* at pandals, with bowl in hand and hunger in starved eyes. The *Hindusthan Standard* dated October 19, 1943, reported a touching tale from Adamdighi in Bagura district (now in Bangladesh). A Muslim boy's body had been found floating in a pond. He was going to the puja in the neighbouring village with his elder brother, in search of *prasaad* but fell exhausted by the wayside. His brother pushed his body into a pond and carried on with his quest for a mouthful.

Fifty years later, when an earthquake rocked Maharashtra on the eve of the Pujas in 1993, the Mohammed Ali Park puja committee decided to raise an extra Rs 50,000 for the earthquake victims. Bagbazar Sarbojanin set up a collection box in front of the pandal for donations from visitors which they would deposit in the Prime Minister's Relief Fund. Ekdalia Evergreen Sarbojanin promised to cut down the budget for immersion and cultural programmes. The *bhog* on Ashtami at the Sealdah Athletic Club was also less elaborate. Yet the cry of the quake-hit did not mar the Rs

Durga Puja. Balthazar Solvyns. *Les Hindous II*
(1810)

Invitation card for the last time the nautch took
place at Sovabazar in 1940

DOORGA PUJAH.

Maharaj Kumar Dharendra Krishna Deb Bahadur
AND
Members of the Sova-Bazar Raj-family.

*With respectful Compliments, request the
favour of* 's
Company to **NAUTCHES** at their residence, on the
7th, 8th, & 9th October 1940 at 9.30 P. M.

SOVABAZAR RAJBARI
30th September 1940.

Last touches being put on the idol at the Saborno Roy Chowdhury puja in
Behala on Panchami night

Offerings for the puja at the Sovabazar *thakurdalan*

A gunshot being fired at the Sovabazar mansion to mark the start of Sandhi Puja

(inset) Family members busy with decorations at the Jaanbazar house of Rani Rashmoni. Portraits of the Rani's guru Shri Ramakrishna and his wife Sarada Ma (on the wall) are also garlanded.

The Bharatmata image of Durga, the national flag in hand, is still worshipped in a few localities of Calcutta, like Bijoygarh

The bamboo framework of a pandal comes up at a roadside

Durga resplendent in golden décor

A mix of the traditional and the contemporary (the "art-Bangla" style) in contrast
to the classic countenance on the book cover

A classic *ekchala* idol in the backdrop of a brightly painted *chalchitra*

Durga in kathakali dance costume

Gigantic hoardings, banners and road dividers rule the streets

A street-corner illumination on a runner, carrying a mail bag over his shoulder, and the poet Sukanta (right) who composed an immortal poem on the runners

A *dhunuchi* dance during the
immersion procession

(inset) Everyone's puja

4-lakh silver jubilee celebrations at Mohammed Ali Park, or dim the lights at Evergreen or stop the giant wheels at the puja fair in Bagbazar.[19] The will to carry on, come what may, has become associated with this festival that serves as a much-awaited release from a stressful routine of work.

If the earthquake in 1993 took place some 2,000 km away in Maharashtra, disaster, in the form of flood fury, had hit closer home in 1978. Twelve districts of Bengal had been inundated, washing away crops and cattle, and triggering an outbreak of cholera. There were some organisers who dispensed with expenditure on lights, microphone and even images, performing a minimalist *ghot* puja instead. But almost all the pujas in the city were held as scheduled and, even in the districts, where the flood waters had not receded, Durga was installed on raised platforms.

And if the organisers were contributing generously, individuals were also pitching in. The *"Kolkatar Korcha"* section of *Anandabazar Patrika* on October 17, 1978, reported one such instance. People had queued up at a collection centre set up by a non-governmental organisation, donating cash and receiving receipts. Among them was a 93-year-old man, a *namabali* (a plain cotton cloth carrying god's name in print) wrapped around his infirm body. He was carrying a few *dhoti*s and saris and had the look of a priest. When his turn came, the old man deposited the clothes and brought out some money from his waistband. "Take these. This is all that I have earned this Puja," he murmured. Overwhelmed at the gesture, the youth at the counter left his chair and touched the old man's feet.

In the shadow of Partition

If Independence unleashed a surge of patriotic euphoria at the pandals, the Partition of Bengal that came with it had different consequences. The thousands of uprooted families that came over from what had overnight turned to East Pakistan brought with them more aspirations than material possessions. While the destitute found shelter in refugee camps in the border districts, those who were a little better off settled on the fringes of the city or in the suburbs. A few years went by before they could find their feet on alien soil. But as soon as they could do so, they set their hearts on a puja of their own. So the second half of the post-Partition decade saw small pujas mushrooming in corners peopled by the former residents of East Bengal. Take Adarsha Pally of Behala, in the far south of Calcutta. Around 60 refugee families had arrived in the area between 1948 and 1952 and bought residential plots at cheap rates. While most found small-time salaried jobs, those who had managed to bring over some capital started their own business. When there was talk of a puja starting in the locality in 1957, the subscriptions ranged from Re 1 to Rs 5 from the first group, which comprised the bulk, to Rs 100 to Rs 150 from the second. The budget in the first few years was a meagre Rs 1,200-Rs 1,500. "The local residents, including my father, did everything themselves, even constructing the pandal," recalls Sumit Basu, a member of the present puja committee.

The story is similar in other "refugee colony" areas. A bulk of the refugees had been rehabilitated in pockets of Dandakaranya at the initiative of the then Chief Minister of West Bengal, Dr B.C. Roy. They were subjected to immense hardship, chopping down trees, clearing land, and creating agricultural plots in the forest. Some got grants from the government in the form of a pair of oxen, a plough and seeds. Writer Narayan Sanyal who was posted in Koraput and Kondagaon, Orissa, in 1959-60 to oversee the process as an executive engineer, remembers seeing Devi Durga being worshipped with the combined resources of four-five villages of settlers.

Clamour for contest crowns

With more and more pujas being organised in closer proximity, people started travelling around to see the images. The *anjali* on Ashtami morning would still be offered to the deity in the locality and the daily *bhog* collected from the local priest, but from then on, Durga Puja would mean an exciting spread of pandals out there waiting to be visited. When the crowd moved from the puja of one locality to another, comparisons were bound to crop up. And once comparisons were made, competition, too, was a natural consequence.

Informal one-upmanship had always existed among the rajas, the *babus*, and even the first generation of community puja organisers. But it took time for the concept to be institutionalised. The first West Bengal government-sponsored competition was organised in 1975. In 1976, Calcutta Police walked into the fray, backing the North Calcutta Co-ordination Committee's effort. This contest, however, stopped in 1977.[20] Corporate enterprise took over in the form of the Asian Paints Sharad Samman in 1985. It was this thoughtfully conceived award—an expression of the growing dissatisfaction with the current trend of frivolous sensationalism—that marked a watershed in the annals of Durga Puja in the modern era.

For the first five years the contest took place in three categories—best image, best pandal and best lighting. But this, as a company-sponsored article explained in an advertisement feature published in *The Telegraph* on October 11, 1994, led to "compartmentalisation" in the organisers' approach, which was "disruptive of the tradition of the Pujas". So a shift was made to three "over-all" awards from 1990.

The significance of the award can be measured only in the light of the context in which it was instituted. A cloud of anarchy had gathered over the festival. Loudspeakers blaring discordant music at ungodly hours, the pandals being used as an extension of the discotheque, even the goddess being made to resemble filmstars by express instructions to the sculptor—all this was indeed reminiscent of some of the worst evils of *babu* puja revisited in a different day and age.

A couple of newspaper articles printed in 1985 convey the degree to which the pujas had sunk. The artist, Paritosh Sen, remembers a Tarzanesque *asura* (demon) swinging from a creeper and about to leap on Durga, sword in hand. If the style of the combat was imported from the West, inspiration for the appearance of the fighters came from closer home. Mahisashura was modelled on Amjad Khan, the villain in the 1970s blockbuster *Sholay*, Durga wore a smile more like that of Hema Malini (the film's glamorous heroine) than divine and Kartik's hair style was a take-off on Amitabh Bachchan, the hero of *Sholay* and the reigning matinee idol of the time.[21] The historian, Radhaprasad Gupta, captures the decadence in a Puja supplement of *Anandabazar Patrika*: "It is difficult to accept the excesses in the decorative lighting in some places. In one puja, I found the pandal drowned in pitch darkness with a crowd waiting outside in silence. Before I could realise what was amiss, the trick started—flashes of various shades of light accompanied by strange sounds splitting the eardrums (referred to as 'quadraphonic' by the organisers). An arrangement inspired by what the Americans call a psychedelic show..." Gupta complains more bitterly about the visible "lack of respect" in the representation of the deity. He recounts an anecdote connected to a puja in Bhowanipur. "A couple of decades ago, organisers of a well-known puja had got an image modelled which, though not unembellished, was totally unclad, with a fitting demeanour. So proud were the organisers of the achievement that they invited a respected personality to their puja. After seeing the image, when the gentleman was getting back into the car in silence, one of them asked for his opinion. 'Capital! Send the lass over to my place in the evening for an hour's chat,' came the sarcastic response (author's translation)."[22]

The new-age contest, carrying the promise of publicity and substantial prizes, emphasised aspects that had taken a backseat in many pujas. The panel of judges comprised eminent citizens from various professions and the parameters of judgment were synergy and harmony among the image, the pandal and the lighting, aesthetic appeal and quality of craftsmanship in all three and a sense of reverence on the pandal premises.

If the organisers welcomed the recognition, people were relieved at the changes that it wrought on the character of the puja. The ambience became more conducive to an act of devotion, harmonious music replaced the din of disturbing decibels, and novelty no longer stooped to the rakish or the ridiculous. Spurred by the success of "Sharad Samman", other corporate bodies, emerging as a pressure group by dint of their sponsorship muscle, started announcing similar contests.

While most stuck to the beaten track in their search for all-round excellence, some of the companies focused on specific aspects of the puja that could be identified with their brand. Thus there emerged a pandal safety award from an

5

Modern Times

Durga Puja today is a socio-cultural event that has long transcended religious contours. For the individual, it is an annual break from the workaday routine, a time to regroup and recharge, a chance to be part of the collective euphoria, to soak in the feel-good in the air, to splurge as though there were no tomorrow. For the city, village or even the house, it is a season to put on a fresh coat of paint, to welcome familiar faces and curious feet, to play itself out on a temporary platform of pleasurable self-gratification that also involves abundant sharing and caring. For the community, it is its best calling card, a stage on which to gather the clan, an occasion to show its kindest all-inviting face. And for the corporate player (the newest entrant on the scene), it is an opportune moment to promote his product through any association with the festival, to come out a winner in the war of the eyeballs, to profit from the consumer's loosened purse strings. It is, in fact, a state of mind on the one hand and on the other a living, breathing physical reality, to which the city wakes up every autumn.

Durga Puja today is big. Bigger than it ever was. And it has spread its geographical wings too, with the festival flagpole being posted in every land where the Bengali Hindu has reached. And in every land thus has begun yet another chapter of this socio-cultural pageantry, rooted in religion but secular in its reach. Technology has aided this journey in ways far beyond those which television (still taking audiences on pandal-hopping trips across the city, to the districts and beyond) could achieve even a decade and a half ago.

Bridge between old and new

In the midst of this onslaught of time-wrought changes, what has lingered on is the family puja. The zamindari system has been abolished in independent India and the title-holders of the Raj are common citizens today. The high-ceilinged colonnaded corridors have left their best days behind and the mansions are generally crumbling. Yet in some of them the pujas carry on, fuelled by the urge to continue with the tradition. "It is not possible to retain the grandeur of our predecessors. But we do our best and beseech the goddess to forgive us our lapses," says Kanu Roy Chowdhury, the 13th descendant of Laxmikanta Majumdar, the founder of the Saborno Roy Chowdhury family. The budget for the puja is about Rs 50,000, with another Rs 25,000 going in the *hom*, the sacred fire that is kept alight through all the days of the puja since the *bodhon*. The family of the founding fathers of the festival in Calcutta spends less on its puja than the neighbouring community puja does on its pandal.

If these pujas are shadows of the past, what makes them special is the fact that they provide a glimpse of history.

Every time the *dhak* drums up a beat for the *bodhon* at the Saborno Roy Chowdhury's or at the Sovabazar Deb's, it is Calcutta's heritage that is receiving a thundering recognition. "We follow every custom that is typical of our puja," says Alok Krishna Deb, eighth in the line from Raja Nabakrishna. Thus, even if a lorry is the favoured mode of transport for the community puja at the adjacent street corner, the idol of the Deb family still travels all the way to the Ganga for immersion on the shoulders of the male members. Mahishasura is always a deep green and Ganesha a blood-red at the Saborno Roy Chowdhury *atchala*, ever since the puja was instituted almost four centuries ago. Work on the Dawn family image starts every year on the holy day of Rathayatra[1] in June-July with the worship of the *kathamo* (wooden structure behind the goddess) and the idol's head is placed on the clay shoulders on Janmashtami, another auspicious occasion in August-September. "We cannot afford to do anything differently," says Ashim Chandra Dawn.

On the one hand, these pujas carry the burden of history. "We receive hundreds of visitors—lots of them tourists from abroad—who ask questions about our traditional rituals. Media persons and chroniclers of the city's history come to us to take notes. We are bound to preserve the past," Deb states.

The other reason seems to stem from faith and superstition. At the Roy Chowdhury puja, animal sacrifice is still practised. The routine reads like this—on Saptami (Day VII): one goat; on Ashtami (Day VIII): two goats; after Sandhi Puja: one goat; on Nabami: nine goats, one buffalo and one pumpkin. "The original stipulation included another buffalo to be sacrificed on Nabami. But once, in the early 1950s, when two buffaloes were being brought from the market in a hackney carriage, one died of suffocation. The bad omen made our forefathers bring the number down to one. We tried to revive the tradition in the early 1970s. That year, a son-in-law of the family died. We have stuck to one buffalo ever since," the 60-year-old Roy Chowdhury recalls.

The winds of change have forced alterations in some traditions. Take the Sovabazar puja. The Scotch Highlander band, sent by the British, which used to precede the Nabapatrika during its bathing procession has given way to a local band party. There is no canon to fire at the start of Sandhi Puja. A gunshot is all there is. The government has put an end to the custom of setting a couple of *neelkantha* birds free on Dashami. The winged creatures, blue-throated like Lord Shiva, were supposed to have acted as messengers to inform the god about his wife's impending return. But the exotic birds, collected from the districts, would die after being set free in an unfamiliar environment, forcing a ban on the 245-year-old practice at the Deb's in 2002. Clay *neelkantha* birds are now brought to "life" by the priest and immersed with the goddess.

A major incentive for continuation of the puja is the gala family reunion. "Our puja is organised by 51 families, all residing in the seven buildings that Nabakrishna Deb's son Rajkrishna built for his seven sons adjacent to his mansion. Add to that the married daughters settled elsewhere, some as far as the United States and the Middle East, who come over for the Pujas. There is hardly space to move in the *thakurdalan* on the four days," laughs Deb. To bring a semblance of order to the flow of visitors, the descendants of Shib Krishna Dawn invite neighbours on Saptami (Day VII), Brahmins on Ashtami (Day VIII) and relatives (numbering around 350) on Nabami (Day IX). "Still, some people decide on their own when to drop in. Surely, they cannot be turned out," explains Dawn.

Durga Puja by itself is a costly proposition and gatherings on such a scale multiply the expenditure. Splits in families, resulting in division of resources, have not helped the cause. Nabakrishna Deb's puja at Sovabazar has had two parallel editions—one at his mansion and the other at the original *thakurdalan* across the road—ever since a Supreme Court ruling in 1806 divided the raja's property to settle a dispute between his sons Gopimohan and Rajkrishna. The Saborno Roy Chowdhurys had branched out to nine pujas, of which six now continue. "Even the five other pujas suffered intermittent breaks. Only the original puja at the *atchala* has maintained a record of continuity," Roy Chowdhury points out. While some houses follow a system of the family units taking turns to foot the expenses for the puja, others believe in collective contribution. Perhaps the Dawn family is among the most organised in this respect. The puja is sponsored by a trust which looks after the earnings of *debuttar*[2] property. The annual expenditure for the puja runs to an impressive Rs 2.5 lakh.

Most of the family pujas may lack the gloss of their cash-rich community counterparts but they are unlikely to fade out. This is mainly because the enthusiasm has percolated to the younger generation. "For the past few years, our boys have even been staging cultural programmes on the occasion," says Dipankar Hazra, of the Jaanbazar family puja. The note of approval is clear in the voice of the 56-year-old descendant of Rani Rashmoni.

Cradle of divinity

Kumortuli. Or the potters' hub. This area in north Calcutta has remained as vital to the festival today as it was in the late eighteenth century, when image-makers from the Nadia district started settling here[3].

Nadia was traditionally home to the image-makers through generations. A few months before the Puja, they would come over to mould the idols at the houses of the babus and return after the festival. Gradually as the number of pujas in the city increased and more work became available, they stayed back, huddled in the same locality by the river Hooghly.

After Partition, there was a sudden spurt in the artisan population as immigrants from across the border invaded the area and set up their studios.

Not much has changed since then. The artisans' world is tucked away in a nondescript lane off a central Calcutta thoroughfare. Pocket after pocket of dingy clay stations lines both its sides as it snakes in and branches out. The congestion has forced many of the better-known image-makers to acquire more space elsewhere. Leaking roof and water-logging create problems when the monsoon lingers. Yet Kumortuli remains the sole port of call for the majority of the puja organisers in the city and the suburbs, or even beyond the Bengal borders.

It is here that the mighty Durga blossoms into shape from a lump of clay and straw and wood in loving hands that have not known any other task. "First, she is my child. Then suddenly she becomes my mother. It makes me nervous. But she guides my fingers," says an old artisan, 72 hoary autumns and generations of idol-making behind him.

Earlier, the puja cycle used to start on the day of Rathyatra[4] when the *kathamo* would be worshipped and orders would start being placed. But now work has to start in April. "This is the age of ready-mades. Some clients come looking for spot buys. So some extra idols have to be kept finished to capture this market," explains one of the artisans.

Kumortuli is not just about the image-makers. The goddess has to be armed, dressed and decorated before she leaves for the pandal. Many families here busy themselves with carvings from the pith of *sola* reed or from silver and gold foil. These are the two predominant media of decoration—the pristine white *sholar saaj* and the gorgeous *daaker saaj*. While *sola* reeds grow in ponds and marshy land, and are very much indigenous, the foils earlier had to be imported from Europe. They came by mail. Hence the name *daaker saaj* (*daak* – mail, *saaj* – dressing). The ingredients for the Devi's décor come from various corners of the state. And the list is long—*sola*, foil, *zari*, jute, clay, straw, tin plates... Some articles come as raw materials, while others, like her sari, weapons and matted hair or the lion's mane and skin, arrive ready for use. The hair and the mane, jute products both, incidentally, are a preserve of workers belonging to the Muslim community.[5]

As *Debipaksha* starts, work here reaches frenetic pace. The cracks on the arm have to be covered with chits of paper. The first coat of paint has to be dried properly for the next coat to be applied. The crown has to be put on without disturbing the carefully pasted locks of hair. And as Sashthi approaches, hundreds of lorries line the main road, waiting in queue to carry the Mother 'home'.

Designs on the Devi

What is the theme of the Puja? The question would have raised indignant eyebrows even in the early 1990s. The daughter's return to her parents. Destruction of evil. Other answers were unlikely. But now there are countless options and the choice of the theme can determine the success of an organiser's annual show. If the household pujas have prided themselves in repeating history and sticking to tradition, the community pujas, as they multiplied in number, resorted to innovative ways to draw the largest crowds.

Size mattered in the earliest stages. This is why Simla Byayam Samiti's 21-foot Durga in 1939 or the gigantic image in Santipur much earlier (mentioned in Chapter IV) found pride of place in contemporary chronicles.

As Kumortuli started experimenting with form, there were new variations in representations of the goddess and the context in which she was placed. If Bharatmata emerged out of popular nationalist sentiments, the separation of the images, breaking up the *ekchala* pattern, was a signature of Gopeshwar Pal, who was called upon to create a difference by the organisers. Once these variations had been accepted, others gained the courage and the freedom to think differently. The changes flowed in parallel streams. While master image-makers like Ramesh Pal, Gorachand Pal, Rakhal Pal and Mohanbanshi Rudrapal gave birth to distinct schools of representation, lesser-known artisans tried their hand at novelties, or even gimmicks, that faded after their four days of fame. (In 1994, for instance, the Goddess hitched a ride on the *Jurassic Park* bandwagon, with a dinosaur appearing beside the lion in the tableau of a puja in Behala, a suburb in Calcutta's extreme south. Priests were aghast at what they called a distortion of Hindu religious mythography. But the organisers, delighted at the long queues of the curious, could not have cared less.)

The major focus of the experiments was obviously on the goddess and her entourage. But from the 1980s onwards, a shift was noticeable towards lighting and illumination effects.

A look at the escalating figures in a prominent central Calcutta puja's budget for lighting (done by SD Electricals, headed by illumination wizard Sridhar Das of suburban Chandannagore, the Kumortuli of lighting[6]) tells the story.

1962 – Rs 2,300
1970 – Rs 5,000
1980 – Rs 45,000
mid-1990s – Rs 1.5 lakh[7]

The state of West Bengal, afflicted by long hours of power cuts round the year, had always been splendidly lit up on the puja nights. With a greater share of the budget being allocated to lighting, the illuminations took on a narrative or tableau-like function. Tiny light-bulbs, called *tuni-bati* in Bengali, were used to illustrate (through pictorial designs) timeless themes like the seasons, the crafts of Bengal, eminent persons, or even contemporary events. Thus the Miss Universe pageant or the terrorist assault on the World Trade Center—everything was staple for the electricians who worked wonders with their tiny lights, often adding moral messages or warnings for their admiring spectators.

After lights, it was the turn of the pandals to take centre stage. In their earliest incarnation, these temporary street-corner shrines would have been a bare framework of bamboo poles draped in cloth spread over tarpaulin. But gradually innovative pandals emerged. Santosh Mitra Square in central Calcutta earned a name for itself by springing extraordinary surprises every year. In 1996, on Netaji's birth centenary, the ship in which, the organisers believe, he had set sail for Japan, was recreated at the park which was its address. "The police had to make special security arrangements, such was the turn-out," recounts an organiser. The next year, cloth and woodwork recreated a recent accident in which a part of a long-distance train fell off a bridge, killing scores of passengers. In Salt Lake, a relatively new and less populated satellite township, huge crowds queued daily to see the *S.S.*

Titanic recreated as a pandal in 1998, the very next year after James Cameron's film *Titanic* swept the Oscars.

Similar wonders, rising to heights of 60 to 70 feet, began to be created in other corners of the city. It was easy to find Washington's White House, Rome's Fountain of Trevi, Kathmandu's Pashupati Nath temple and Agra's Taj Mahal at a stone's throw from each other, all crafted by decorators who had never stepped out of Bengal and had only photographs in magazines or books to guide them. What was most amazing about these illusionistic masterpieces was that they simulated the appearance of marble and stone with nothing more than cloth, bamboo and cardboard. Experiments would be (and still are) carried out in unusual media, such as soap, medicine bottles, clay cups, old bakelite record discs, biscuits and red chilli, but the 1960s and 1970s fad of creating the images themselves out of these unusual substances seems to have passed. The deity is now left well alone, to be modelled in the traditional clay, while the pandal provides the space where novel ideas take shape.

From the mid-90s, one might note a concerted effort to weave all aspects of the puja into a harmonious whole. The resulting creation would deliver a message, tell a story or recreate a way of life. This is what is called theme-based puja or, in common parlance, theme puja.

Thus when an organiser in Dhakuria, south Calcutta, chooses a 'kathakali dance village' for a theme, the local park becomes a corner of Kerala complete with its backwaters, palm trees and a couple of live ducks swimming in the canal, dug out just for the festival. Mud huts are constructed where kathakali dancers put on their elaborate make-up in full view of the visitors before ascending the stage at one side of the pandal for performances. Craftsmen sit and design Keralan handicrafts, to be sold to interested visitors. Even the images

Giving shape to the basic structure of the idol in straw

Casts of the Goddess' face taken in clay being dried

The paintbrush being applied to the idols, defying the rain god,
in the Kumortuli alleys

The vital task of drawing the eyes

A pandal at Santosh Mitra Square modelled on a ship

The controversial bifurcation of Eastern Railway, headquartered in Calcutta, embodied in a pandal at Santosh Mitra Square in 2002

The Fountain of Trevi in Rome, created at Khidirpur (west Calcutta)

The goddess in the Fountain of Trevi pandal, modelled in the Roman style

The goddess in the clay cup pandal.
The background décor also uses cups

ॐ·ॐ

The biggest crowd-puller in recent times –
a pandal made of 1.5 million clay cups
(*kulhars*) of different sizes in Bosepukur,
Kasba, in 2001

A pandal on the theme of pressure of education on children

A paean to peace, in the Buddhist style, in the year of the Iraq aggression (2003).
All the gods, weaponless, clasp their hands in prayer as Mahishasura begs
for an end to war

A fortress, complete with cannon, on the outskirts of Calcutta

Durga Puja at Jersey City in the USA. A basketball court is hired for the weekend festivity

An artist's impression of Durga of
the future on a calendar

A mini idol at a Kumortuli studio,
ready to take off for London

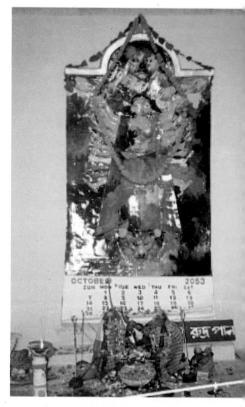

of the deities are in kathakali costume. Zonal lighting is used, under the guidance of a theatre professional, to create the look of a sleepy village, lulled by recordings of the drone of crickets and the croaking of frogs played on concealed amplifiers. The research for this puja took about two months, including a trip to Kerala, says the puja committee president.

A film studio can be recreated in an alley in Barisha, Behala. The entrance is lined with posters and negatives of still shots of Indian films which have used Durga Puja—from the black and white *Pather Panchali* and *Nayak* to the technicolour *Devdas* and *Utsab*. The passage leads to the studio floor where elaborate shooting equipment is mounted in front of the goddess—movie camera, reflectors, multi-10 lights... The inner walls of the pandal are lined with sound-absorbing grass boards. A screen displays the puja-centred sequences from the films. During *anjali* (offerings) or *aarati* (greeting of the goddess), the ritual is shot on camera and the footage shown later in the day on the pandal projector.

Some of the most remarkable theme pujas are conceived as works of art. The organisers of the Bakul Bagan Road puja in Bhowanipore, south Calcutta, have established a tradition of requesting some of the most famous living artists of Bengal to create the image of the goddess, in a chosen setting, each year. Memorable creations were produced by the late Meera Mukherjee, one of the greatest of modern sculptors, and even by Isa Mohammad, a Muslim who was then principal of the Government Art College.

Art and craft of a particular region—terracotta panels or lac dolls, dokra figurines or Madhubani paintings—come up as motif of an entire puja complex, bringing artists from remote corners into the limelight and giving encouragement to the craftsmen and their art form.

Clearly, such planning is beyond the capability of the pandal-decorator, the image-maker or the electrician. This is where the theme-maker has come in. This is a person who formulates the ideas, instructs the artisans and oversees the work. While many people with a creative bent of mind but coming from unrelated professional backgrounds take to theme-making during the pujas, art directors of films and art college graduates are also becoming involved with the pujas in large numbers. For both groups, it is a job on the side, not as yet their principal profession. But it is a task that shapes the look of a particular puja and decides its fate on the popularity scales and the awards lists.

Consumer carnival

Durga Puja is the biggest business event on the calendar in Bengal. Money in multiples of millions changes hands as people save up through the year to indulge themselves during this period. It is a tradition for employers to make bonus payments before the Puja as a goodwill gesture to employees. For the West Bengal government alone, the annual payment in bonus and festival advance adds up to Rs 70 crore.[8]

Shopping has always been an integral part of the puja. Garments to gadgets, cars to jewellery, no product is denied the benison of the buyer. ORG-Marg, a leading market research company, pegs consumer spending estimates in the city in two months of the festival period at over Rs 350 crore.[9]

Earlier, people would even travel to the city from the suburbs at this time of the year to pick up the fashionable best for their family and friends. In 1927, the Eastern Bengal Railway ran a train called Pujo Bazaar Special for a month before the festival, that reached a variety of ware from the city—clothes, cosmetics, culinary utensils and the like—to consumers in remote areas. From August 31 to October 1, the train with three compartments travelled 1,124¼ miles, stopping at 20 stations (often for days, depending on the response) on the way. The average daily turnout at each station was 5,000 and articles worth more than Rs 1 lakh were sold.[10]

The shopping festival that is the Puja has spawned an entire genre of products, called Puja specials. After all, it is common commercial sense to push a commodity when the consumer has the money and is in the mood to splurge. New music albums are released during this time, as are special numbers of magazines.

Puja has its own brand of music called *agamani* that heralds the home-coming of the daughter of the Himalayas. These songs could be heard from itinerant troubadours in villages with the approach of Mahalaya. But the festival was used as an occasion to launch an album for the first time in September 1914. The artiste who gave voice to two *kirtan*s on the two sides of the first Gramophone Company of India Puja album was Manada Sundari Dassi. That year, 17 records, each costing three rupees and 12 annas, were released.

Soon it became common practice for music companies to target all their major releases around this time. Booklets were distributed from music stores, containing photographs of the artistes and lyrics of the new songs, which would also be broadcast on the radio. Countless evergreen hits, like Hemanta Mukherjee's *Runner*, *Gnayer Badhu* and *Palkir Gaan*, were originally part of the Puja bouquet of the respective years. With the exit of the great names in Bengali music, the quality of original songs released on the occasion has gone down, though the number of releases has multiplied manifold. Technology has made cutting an album an easier and cheaper proposition. Such is the opportunistic lure of the moment that many small recording companies now spring to life during the Pujas to bring out a few albums and sink into oblivion immediately afterwards. "Sales in the festive season are still far higher than at any point of time round the year but the new songs are not awaited with as much eagerness as they were till the 1970s," points out S.F. Karim, business manager of Saregama India Ltd, which has taken over the monolithic HMV label from the Gramophone Company of India.

If the music does not generate as much excitement as before, Puja literature remains high on popularity stakes. In fact, the Puja-special magazines have become as integral to the occasion as new clothes are, rapidly increasing in circulation ever since *Anandabazar Patrika* brought out a separate magazine, priced at two annas, in 1926.[11] Earlier, a few extra pages in journals, containing stories or novels, designated as Puja literature, were all that there was. But once the start was made, in the next two decades other magazines and newspapers—*Desh*, *Dainik Basumati*, *Jugantar* and *Hindusthan*—came out with Puja magazines featuring a feast of stories and poems and essays, commissioned specially for the occasion.[12] A pointer to the popularity is the sharp rise in the number of pages and the price of *Anandabazar Patrika*'s puja edition. By 1935, it was a 284-page book, carrying a price tag of eight annas. Today there are Puja specials to suit every pocket and preference, including a few in English to cater to the huge non-Bengali population in the city which soaks in the Puja spirit as well.

Theatres and regional films also debut on the stage and screen respectively to draw in the vacationing hordes. So much so that the theatres, in their heydays, would hold multiple shows, often through the night, on Mahalaya and the big four days. Ticket prices would be higher and people from even the districts would flock to watch doyens like Sisir Bhaduri, Ahindra Chowdhury, Chhabi Biswas and Saraju Debi in action. If the theatres are no longer a chosen destination, the movie halls are, with film producers targeting the Fridays around the Puja for their releases.

Travel is another sector that receives a festive boost. The family reunion that Durga Puja occasions has always generated a sizeable travelling traffic. If many are homing in, lots of others are also flying or chugging out to enjoy the long vacation. At the beginning of the 20th century, Great Eastern Hotel was advertising "an enormous stock of travelling requisites—steel trunks, Hat Boxes, Gladstone Bags...suits, cigars..." under the heading "Poojah Holidays, 1900".[13] The Bengal-Nagpur Railway was offering return tickets at single fare and prescribing its tracks as "The way to travel for your Pooja Holidays to Puri By the Sea" (*The Statesman*, September 1905).[14]

R. Pearson, in his 1933 publication *Eastern Interlude: A Social History of the European Community in Calcutta,* quotes a poem, *Song of the Durga Poojah,* published in a contemporary city newspaper. This is the concluding stanza:

The church, the mart, the court of law,
The __ everywhere's deserted;
The very crows have ceased to caw,
And Echo's broken-hearted:
The palac'd town in silence stands,
For none are left in it to jaw; —
All creeds, or, as we say, all hands
Being off for the Doorga Poojah.
Sing tol de rol.

Now, during the Pujas, the city welcomes an influx of visitors—both seasonal and daily. While the seasonal ones are family members returning home on vacation, an onslaught of daily visitors is witnessed on the Puja days. People come from the districts in groups and roam from pandal to pandal, giving business to Metro, the underground railway, which runs through the night to cater to this crowd. Tour operators, including the tourism department of the state government, organise conducted trips to facilitate visits to celebrated pujas. This is boom time for heritage tourism, an emerging vista. Visitors from abroad (both foreigners and non-resident Indians) are served a platter that adds an exotic taste of the city and its culture through bullock cart and tram rides, dance programmes, local cuisines and visits to Mother Teresa's home and Victoria Memorial alongside the pandal-hopping and participation in *sindur khela*, specially organised for them. For local residents seeking a break, the travel agencies chalk out package tours, covering destinations near and far, from Mumbai to Malaysia.

Promotions are imperative to reach all this communication to the consumer. In September 1891, Eroom & Co of Dhurrumtollah Street makes an announcement "Important to Native Gentlemen!" "Doorga Poojas are Coming," a trumpeteer in a circus suit blew a horn on the pages of *The Statesman*, "We have just received from Calicut an assortment of the famous Basel Mission Cotton Tweeds…"[15] The trumpet-blowing intensified as the community puja became bigger and brighter. Geoffrey Moorhouse in his 1971 publication *Calcutta*, writes how "As the Puja approaches, the shopkeepers of Calcutta go dotty with offers of ten per cent discounts on all purchases…".[16]

Today, festival marketing has flourished far beyond the ten per cent discount that shopkeepers used to pull out of their hats. Marketing campaigns are worked out months in advance to create the hype and stoke the fire of consumerism. Footwear company Bata showed the way by linking the occasion with its product through the memorable slogan *Pujoy Chai Notun Juto* (Wanted new shoes for the Pujas). "There was a time when we would register as much as 40 per cent of our sales during this season. Early in the year, we would check the almanac to find out what the Devi's mode of transport would be that Puja and plan our advertisements using that information," reminisces Dilip Chattopadhyay, a former marketing manager of Bata.[17] "Even today, Durga Puja is the single largest sales opportunity in eastern India," says Chirantan Chandran, an advertising professional handling the shoe major's account for the past 12 years.

Banners, festoons and stalls on the puja premises have long vied for the pandal-hoppers' attention. Now companies want their products not only to be seen and sold, but also to blot out rival brands. So a cola giant would pump in money for a puja only if the organiser agrees to keep other soft drinks away from the pandal premises. Similar clauses would be clamped by ice cream majors or newspaper companies.

The sponsorship war, so far restricted to the street corners, has now scaled the boundary walls and reached the housing complexes. These small-scale pujas organised by residents of multi-storeyed apartments carry the intimate spirit of cooperation of a handful of neighbours that the *baroari* form had started out with.

In a move that may bring about a radical change in the character of these pujas in future, sponsors are introducing intra-complex contests—*dhunuchi* (censer) dance, sit-and-draw, *diya* (lamp) lighting and the like—and even funding the events at chosen apartment complexes. The parameters of judging the best apartment pujas, of course, are different from those for the community puja and stress on a participative ambience. While the well-organised routine of events inspires greater involvement in the residents, it has also introduced these hitherto cloistered pockets to cash prize and publicity.

For the community puja, the budget spiral has been steep. In 1931, the Bagbazar Sarbojanin committee collected Rs 3,203 and 25 paise. They could not spend the entire amount and had a surplus of Rs 79 and 10 annas. In 1993, the budget for the same puja was Rs 4.05 lakh.[18] In 2003, it doubled, reaching a figure of about Rs 8 lakh. "The corporate presence has increased manifold," admits Benoy Dhar, the treasurer of the Park Circus Sarbojanin. The USP of this Puja is the fair—a permanent fixture since the 1960s —which continues for a fortnight after the Pujas, featuring stalls from bangle-makers to cola giants.

It is easy to explain the eagerness of advertisers to make their presence felt at the prominent pujas. The daily footfall at each pandal runs into multiples of thousands. Park Circus, for instance, recorded 12,000 visitors till the stroke of midnight on Ashtami (Day VIII) in 2002, while Jodhpur Park Sarbojanin welcomed 18,000 in the same period.[19] The figures could only have increased as the night advanced.

A corollary to the inflow of sponsorship money is the decreasing dependence on subscriptions from local residents. "Till the Eighties, the mainstay of every puja was door-to-door collection. Now it accounts for barely 10 per cent of our capital. The money comes from advertisements in the puja souvenir and sponsorships for banners, posters and stalls. Whatever collection the boys do is to keep the locals happy," Sumanta Roy, the president of Jodhpur Park

Sarbojanin Puja Committee, points out. A long trip in time from Guptipara and the 12 friends,[20] indeed.

Beyond the borders

Durga Puja crossed the borders of Bengal centuries before *baroari* puja was born in Calcutta. Varanasi, the sacred city on the bank of the Ganga in north India, has long been a favourite get-away of the Bengalis. In the 18th century, the aristocrats were in the habit of travelling to Varanasi and holding Durga Puja there for piety's sake.[21]

In Delhi, the first puja is said to date back to the mid-19th century with the worship of a Dakshina-Kali idol. But the temple was destroyed during the uprising of 1857. Durga Puja staged a revival at the Roshanpuri Kali temple with the worship of a symbolic *ghot* in 1910. With the shift of the country's capital from Calcutta to Delhi in 1911, the number of Bengalis there increased and Durga Puja proliferated.[22] In Mumbai, the Puja is said to have staged a debut in the fag end of the 19th century at the hands of the goldsmiths settled in Kalbadevi.[23] Bengalis who migrated to Mumbai to work in the Hindi film industry in the 1950s, 60s and 70s started some of the most popular pujas there.

Durga Puja is now held in every major city of India. The ten-armed goddess has set sail across the seven seas and conquered the five continents as well. Religious centres, like the Ramakrishna Mission, played a key role in the spread, especially in England and America.

Durga Puja did face resistance in some areas. Photographs of the goddess printed on Indian newspapers were smeared with black ink at the airport customs counter of an Islamic country in the Middle East, where puja organisers had to smuggle in mini idols tucked in their personal luggage.

Hindus in neighbouring Bangladesh threatened to boycott all ceremony and perform only a minimal *ghot* puja in protest against communal atrocities in 1993.

But in other countries, the Puja has spread with the rise in the Bengali Hindu expatriate population. The year 2004, for instance, marked Durga's debut in Vietnam. All of 30 Bengalis gathered at a local temple of a South Indian deity in Saigon with a Vietnamese priest who was coached in mantras from a methodology booklet brought over from Calcutta. Puja was offered to a small terracotta figurine belonging to the home altar of one of the organisers.[24] The story of the start is similar in most countries. The United States, with a high concentration of Bengalis and mushrooming community pujas, is an interesting case study.

Till the 1960s, the majority of Indians in the United States were associated with education. It was natural in such circumstances that Saraswati would be the first from the pantheon to make an entry into hostel rooms, even if it meant worshipping a picture of the goddess of learning on the designated day, in the absence of an idol. In the 1970s and 1980s as the surge of immigration started, there was a felt need for forums for community gatherings. Thus Bengali clubs and associations were formed across the country. After staging a variety of cultural programmes, they gained enough confidence to think of organising the greatest show on earth for Bengalis.

Durga Puja had already started on a low key on individual initiative. In 1966, a picture of the goddess and the symbolic *ghot* were worshipped in the community hall of an apartment in New York.[25] Similar small-scale pujas could have taken place around that time in other parts of the country as well.

But it took collective enterprise to ship in an image and start a puja. The year was 1970 and the organiser the East

Coast Durga Puja Committee, New York.[26] Dodge Hall in the Columbia University complex hosted Bengalis from across the country for a gala gathering. They went back to their cities inspired to launch their own festival.

In their earliest avatars, these pujas were small intimate get-togethers where the invitations were personalised, the arrangement simple and the wives happily cooked the community meals, taken together at the puja venue. Now, with the numbers explosion after the Silicon Valley boom, the festive schedule and other details are floated on the association's website for all to see and visit the puja at their convenience.

How different are Pujas abroad from their counterparts at home? A lot. There are no red-letter days on a foreign country's calendar to mark out the festival and Durga Puja does not bring with it a vacation as it does in Bengal. So the four days of rituals often have to be compressed into a weekend. Says Abhas Bhattacharya, one of the most popular priests in the New York Bengali circuit: "We do not heed the actual *tithi* (prescribed auspicious moment in the almanac). All the rituals follow one after the other." There are no street-corner pandals; community halls or auditoriums are rented to host the Devi. "We have to be careful while throwing the flowers at the goddess during *pushpanjali* (floral offering) so as not to spoil the carpet and incur the wrath of the hall authorities," laughs Surjamukhi Chatterjea Moulik, a software professional settled in Chicago. Participation in many places comes as a package, with entry, community meals and cultural programmes all clubbed under one ticket. The food usually comes from restaurants. "Who will cook for 400 people?" reasons Arkadev Chatterjea, a former researcher at Cornell University who used to organise the puja under the Milonee banner at Arvada, Colorado, in the late 1990s.

Priesthood is not a career option abroad and it would be self-taught amateurs doing the job. "Their pronunciation of the Sanskrit *mantras* (incantations) can be quite funny," Chatterjea adds.

Visitors to the pujas comprise four categories—old-timers who migrated decades ago, new-comers who are mostly students, temporary workers who come on short-term assignments, second-generation Indians who would have problems speaking Bengali and often feel a little left-out, and non-Indian spouses from mixed-race marriages who turn up dressed in full Bengali regalia.

Importing the idol is a key concern. Bhattacharya recalls: "A friend had once brought over 32 kg of clay from the Ganga (the best variety for clay models) along with a mould and then made the image here." Now, of course, the option of shipment is there and orders come to Kumortuli from across the Atlantic. Artist Amarnath Ghosh, who specialises in idols carved out of *sola* pith, received as many as 18 orders from abroad in 2003. The US accounted for nine while other orders came from England, Italy, Canada, Malaysia, Austria and Belgium. Three came from Finland, Sweden and Denmark, making them the first exports to Scandinavian countries in Ghosh's 25 years in the trade.

For logistical reasons, the images worshipped abroad are much smaller and are not immersed every year. "We neatly pack up the idols and store the packet in someone's house till the next Puja. Given that we have a *sola* pith idol, a wrapping of a dried mud-soaked cloth ensures longevity," says Bhattacharya, the New York priest. New images are ordered once every five or six years.

If Bengalis are setting up cultural base on new pastures, they are also getting involved in a rerun of traditional trans-border rivalry. "After years of watching Indians hosting Durga

Puja, non-resident Bangladeshi Hindus have started their own festival. So keen is the competition that I receive calls from Bangladeshi organisers in the US urging me to make their idol better than that of their Indian neighbours," Ghosh says.

Talk of the East Bengal-Mohun Bagan duel[27] being fought out on a Puja pitch!

Conclusion

Whither Puja

An empty garage. Inside, on the distant wall, hangs a calendar, open at October 2053. A face—of Durga—juts out from its surface. This was image-maker Pradip Rudrapaul's cynicism caught in clay at a pandal in Behala, south Calcutta, predicting the look of the Puja in future.

The demon-slaying Devi is gradually losing ground to the peripherals. "Once upon a time, people would come to see the idol. But those days are long gone. Other things are now played up to catch their eye," the young artiste smiles wryly.

The attention may have well and truly shifted from religiosity and rites. Yet it would be unwise to miss the strong positive note in the trends that have emerged in the Puja of the 21st century. The awards have guaranteed an awareness among the organisers about social and civic issues. The parameters for assessment charted out for every contest prove how the judges look beyond the sheen. Safety, traffic norms, arrangement for senior citizens to view the deity, concern for noise pollution, first aid facilities, provisions to search for lost mates, drinking water supply, fire precautions, toilet facilities, waste management procedures and more are what score in their book. And the focus is not just on the four days of festivities. Bonus points are added for welfare activities in other months of the year. The fallout of this philanthropic push is obvious. From Santosh Mitra Square in central Calcutta to Bosepukur Sitala Mandir in the south-east, puja organisers speak in one voice: "The biggest share of our budget is spent on social services round the year." Even if this is frowned upon as claptrap, the good work gets done. Surely, a gain has emerged out of the gloss.

Another overwhelming feature is the way technology is logging into the festival. It is now possible to offer *anjali* on the Net, with websites dedicated to Durga Puja keeping e-flowers, e-garlands and e-incense sticks ready for those failing to make it to the pandal on Ashtami (Day VIII) morning. The recorded voice chanting the *mantra*s to the devotee replaces the priest in lands where the Devi has not set foot on. Virtual pandal tours are also possible through pictures uploaded on such sites through the Puja days.

For those wanting to make it to the pandal but wary of the crowd, cellphone companies are coming forward with offers which would help their subscribers cut the queue, thanks to corporate tie-ups with the puja organisers. *Bhog* (the holy food offered first to the goddess and then partaken of by devotees) is also getting delivered at the doorstep through orders over cellphone text messages.

If such trends gain ground, there is a risk of a division of the privileged and the non-privileged on what had so far been a level revelry field. An opinion poll was conducted during Puja 2003 in a newspaper on whether tickets should be introduced at pandals to allow the buyers to view the goddess without the wait and the sweat. Though a handful agreed, the motion faced stiff resistance from the majority.

An artisan who won a Puja award for excellence in 2003 made a comment at the prize-distribution ceremony which is at once curious and a correct pointer to the spirit in which the festival is taken. "Winning the Sharad Samman," he said, "is like winning the World Cup".

Organising a Puja today means much more than collection of the list of things required for worship, or rather the list has changed radically in character from the time when kings sent out messengers near and far in search of every item prescribed by the priest. So much so that a couple of event management companies have come into existence, offering package deals to take care of all one's organisational worries—from sending out press invitations to preparing the daily *bhog*. This distances the community from its own *baroari* puja in terms of the personal touch but it must be conceded that the event today is indeed bigger than what any 12 friends would be capable of putting together, if they want to come into the reckoning as a crowd-puller.

Durga Puja today has become a carnival, full of bright lights and festive cheer. The way it has laid itself open to the tides of popular culture and the consequences thereof do have critics. With commercialisation and urbanisation of the festival, the outward paraphernalia have become a lot more elaborate and have taken precedence over much of the familiar emotions that were at the heart of its primitive attraction. The identification of the goddess as a daughter is perhaps what had strengthened the emotional bond with the people, which in turn paved the way for the phenomenal growth in the festival's popularity. In fact, the lore surrounding Durga's four-day visit reflected a common desire of every family—a visit of the married daughter, an occurrence rare enough in the days of slow-moving transport, uncertain roads and patriarchal rigours of a joint family. Devotion, too, has lost its mystic aura. As historian of culture Chidananda Dasgupta points out, "...(The priests) have become an anachronism tolerated by young enthusiasts as an unavoidable appendage of the fun and frolic... that the Pujas represent to them. Nobody understands the Sanskrit slokas they recite (sometimes including themselves) and there is little attempt at translation... Perforce, their ceremony is at once central to the activity and peripheral to the consciousness."[1]

Though piety may have taken a toss, the popularity makes up for it. The Puja is a successful survival story albeit with a paradigm shift. The conversion of the devout worship of a deity to a fun-filled extravaganza has allowed it to retain its popularity in an age which is actively sceptical about and distancing itself from the trappings of conventional religious practices.

At the same time, by inviting all communities within its fold, enabling and energising the mirth-making faculties of the people at large, Durga Puja has had a beneficial and harmonising effect on society. For that alone, one can surely be grateful to the goddess.

Notes

Chapter 1

1. There is a single reference to Rama having performed a puja at Lord Brahma's advice to attain victory in the *Ramayana* authored by sage Valmiki, in the section, 'Lankakando', Chapter 83, sloka no 34. See Haripada Acharya, *Mahalaya Theke Bijoya* (Shree Ramkrishna Mission Ashram, Narendrapur, 1991) p 12. Krittivasa (born c. 1432) was a Bengali poet, hailing from Phulia in Nadia district, who composed a Bengali version of the *Ramayana*, using other religious texts as additional sources, in the mid-fifteenth century. See Swami Prajnanananda, *Mahishasuramardini-Durga* (Shree Ramkrishna Vedanta Math, Calcutta, 1990) p 246.

2. According to *Matsyapurana*, the divine day spans from the 11th day of the full moon cycle in Magha* (mid January to mid-February) to the 11th day of the half moon cycle in Asharha* (mid-June to mid-July). The dark hours for the gods are the rest of the year—from Shravana* (mid-July to mid-August) to Poush* (mid-December to mid-January).

   *Months in the Bengali calendar which follows the lunar cycle.

3. Sukumari Bhattacharji, *Legends of Devi* (Disha Books, Orient Longman: Mumbai, 1998) p 26. *Devi Bhagabata*, *Devi Rahasya Tantra* and *Skandhapurana* mention the Devi killing a demon called Durgo or Durgam.

4. Hansanarayan Bhattacharya, *Hinduder Debdebir Udbhab O Kromobikash*, Vol 2 (Pharma KLM, Calcutta, 1978) p 138-139.

5. Sukumari Bhattacharji, *Legends of Devi* (Disha Books, Orient Longman: Mumbai, 1998) p 45-46. Also Hansanarayan Bhattacharya, *Hinduder Debdebir Udbhab O Kromobikash*, Vol 2 (Pharma KLM, Calcutta, 1978) p 144-145.

6. J. Muir, *Original Sanskrit Texts on the Origin and History of the People of India, their Religion and Institutions*. Quoted in Subodh Kapoor (ed.), *The Hindus: Encyclopaedia of Hinduism*, Vol 5 (Cosmo Publications, Delhi, 2000) p 326-27.

7. Vettam Mani, *Puranic Encyclopaedia* (Motilal Banarsidass, Delhi, 1975) p 695.

8. Sukumari Bhattacharji, *Legends of Devi* (Disha Books, Orient Longman: Mumbai, 1998) p 98.

9. Vettam Mani, *Puranic Encyclopaedia* (Motilal Banarsidass, Delhi, 1975) p 449.

10. Hansanarayan Bhattacharya, *Hinduder Debdebir Udbhab O Kromobikash*, Vol 3 (Pharma KLM, Calcutta, 1980) p 70. Also Purba Sengupta, 'Shree O Sampader Devi Laxmi', *Bartaman*, October 4, 1998.

Chapter 2

1. Durga Puja is written about in the greatest detail in *Devipurana*, *Kalikapurana*, *Matsyapurana* and *Brihannandikeshwarpurana*.

2. The puja can be held for a longer period, the maximum being 16 days. The period depends on the day on which one takes the *sankalpa* or the formal resolution to worship the goddess. In most pujas now, this is done on Day 6 of the divine fortnight of the full moon, ending the proceedings on Day 10, making it a four-day affair. But there are provisions to take the resolution on Day nine of the previous fortnight, taking the festival day-count to 16. This happens only in a few family pujas now.

3. There are 16 ingredients and religious ceremonies that are required for Durga Puja—seat, welcoming, water to wash

feet, offerings, water for purification, sweet oblation, water to wash face and mouth, articles for ablution, clothings, cover, perfume, flowers, incense, lamp, altarage and worship. But there are provisions for a range of short cuts in *Kalikapurana* when all this cannot be arranged for. The next shortened step is puja with five articles—perfume, flowers, incense, lamp and altarage. If this too is hard to find, then the minimum is flowers and water. But in times of peril, like famine or war, when nothing is at hand, devotion suffices.

4. Raghunandan, a resident of Nabadwip, in Nadia district, is known to have authored three books on Durga Puja methodology—*Durgotsavtatva*, *Durgapujatatva* and *Krityatatva*—which are followed by priests today. He has comprehensively quoted both the Puranas and works of predecessors. Other scholars have penned Puja methodologies as well, Pundit Ramesh Shastri, who took on the job for Raja Kangsanarayan of Taherpur, being one. But none matches Raghunandan in acceptance.

5. An invocation of the gods to the Devi in *Markandeyapurana* indicates the importance of the *ghot*. "O you, the Supremely Powerful, who cradles the universe to thyself, for you are the Earth. And as water, you suckle and nourish the universe…" (author's translation)

6. In 1993, the two had deduced different dates for Mahasaptami, leading to wide-spread confusion, as the Union government declares its holidays following Visuddha Siddhanta while the West Bengal government follows the Gupta Press almanac, which belongs to the Surya Siddhanta school. Earlier, in 1982, the Centre declared Puja holidays in September based on Visuddha Siddhanta. But Gupta Press and PM Bakchi almanacs set the dates in October. After much speculation, the then Chief Minister, Jyoti Basu, adhered to the popular choice.

Chapter 3

1. Rajasuya Yagna was a great ritualistic sacrifice performed by rulers who aspired to the title of emperor.

2. Ashwamedha Yagna involved a horse sacrifice. A horse of pure breed was allowed to run loose for a year and an army followed it. All the territory that the horse could pass through uninterrupted became its master's. Whoever stopped the horse became involved in war with the escorting army. The sacrificial ritual was performed on its return.

3. Raja Jagatnarayan of Bhaduria followed soon after Kangshanarayan, spending around Rs 9 lakh. But his Durga puja was of the vernal variety. Some accounts mention Raja Ganesh performing Durga Puja in the 15th century during his seven-year rule in Bengal to unite the Hindus. But it is Kangshanarayan who finds the greatest support as the founder of Durga Puja in modern times.

4. Bimal Chandra Ghosh, *Durga Puja Sekal Theke Ekal* (Ramkrishna Vivekananda Institute of Research and Culture, Calcutta, 1986) p 191-192.

5. Shripantho, *Smritir Pujo* (Punoshcho, Calcutta, 2003) p 45-46.

   Samachar Darpan is the first Bengali weekly newspaper, founded by Rev. Joshua Marshman and his son John Clark Marshman, in 1818. They also issued *The Friend of India* (referred to later) as a monthly magazine, which was incorporated in *The Statesman*, one of Bengal's leading English dailies at present.

6. "From the time of the first creation of the office, 1720, down to 1756, the zemindar had a native deputy, known as the black deputy or black zamindar. One Govindram Mittre filled the office for the whole of the period, and according to Holwell's report commited 'sundry abuses and depredations'." (Editorial note in Prankrishna Dutta, *Kolikatar Itibritto O Onnanyo Rachana*, p 175). Also see Note 9.

7. The ornaments were taken off before immersion in the river. The Dawn family history, entitled *Dawn Bangsho Brittanto* by Haradhan Dutta, mentions how led by an urge to score over the Dawns, Prince Dwarkanath Tagore, another wealthy babu and grandfather of poet-philosopher Rabindranath

Tagore, once immersed the image at his house with the gold ornaments on. (Quoted in *Smritir Pujo*, p 26).

8. Bimal Chandra Ghosh, *Durga Puja Sekal Theke Ekal* (Ramkrishna Vivekananda Institute of Research and Culture, Calcutta, 1986) p 112.

9. An East India Company post, carrying with it the duties of collector and judge.

10. Binoy Ghosh, *Kolkata Shohorer Itibritto* (Bak Sahitya, Calcutta, 1975) p 318.

11. Binoy Ghosh, *Kolkata Shohorer Itibritto* (Bak Sahitya, Calcutta, 1975) p 322.

12. Binoy Ghosh, *Kolkata Shohorer Itibritto* (Bak Sahitya, Calcutta, 1975) p 320.

13. Gopimohan was Nabakrishna's elder brother's son whom he adopted.

14. Bimal Chandra Ghosh, *Durga Puja Sekal Theke Ekal* (Ramkrishna Vivekananda Institute of Research and Culture, Calcutta, 1986) p 154-155.

15. Bimal Chandra Ghosh, *Durga Puja Sekal Theke Ekal* (Ramkrishna Vivekananda Institute of Research and Culture, Calcutta, 1986) p 114.

16. Quoted in P.C. Bagchi (ed.), Chapt IV entitled "The Social Life in Calcutta", *The Second City of the Empire: The 25th Session of the Indian Science Association* (Calcutta, 1938).

17. P. Thankappan Nair (ed.), *Calcutta in the 19th Century* (Pharma KLM, Calcutta, 1989) p 192.

18. Shripantho, *Smritir Pujo* (Punoshcho, Calcutta, 2003) p 39-40.

19. P. Thankappan Nair (ed.), *Calcutta in the 19th Century* (Pharma KLM, Calcutta, 1989) p 88-89.

20. P. Thankappan Nair (ed.), *Calcutta in the 19th Century* (Pharma KLM, Calcutta, 1989).

21. Shibshankar Bharati, "Sekaler Saradotsab", *Bartaman*, October 13, 2002.

22. Bimal Chandra Ghosh, *Durga Puja Sekal Theke Ekal* (Ramkrishna Vivekananda Institute of Research and Culture, Calcutta, 1986) p 90.

23. *Bengal Spectator*, October 5, 1842. Extract printed in Ranabir Ray Choudhury (ed.), *Glimpses of Old Calcutta (Period 1836-1850)* (Nachiketa Publications, Bombay, 1978) p 68.

24. Bimal Chandra Ghosh, *Durga Puja Sekal Theke Ekal* (Ramkrishna Vivekananda Institute of Research and Culture, Calcutta, 1986) p 110.

Chapter 4

1. Dr P.C. Bagchi (ed.), "The Social Life in Calcutta", Chapter IV, in *The Second City of the Empire: The 25th Session of The Indian Science Congress Association* (Calcutta, 1938).

2. Shripantho, *Smritir Pujo* (Punoshcho, Calcutta, 2003) p 22.

3. Jaya Chaliha and Bunny Gupta, "Durga Puja in Calcutta", in Sukanta Chaudhuri (ed.) *The Living City*, Vol 2 (Oxford University Press, Calcutta, 1990), p. 332. The writers mention a plaque at Bindeshwaritala shrine dating the event to 1761. In the absence of definite records, it is best not to put an exact date to it.

4. Binoy Ghosh, *Paschimbanger Sanskriti*, Vol. 2 (Prakash Bhavan, Calcutta, 1978), pp 279-80. Ghosh mentions a list of articles used in the second year of the Guptipara puja being found in the residence of the Mukhopadhyays, which indicates the first year to have been 1759-60, earlier than what *The Friend of India* surmises.

5. Kaliprasanna Singha, *Hutom Pnyachar Naksha*, ed. Arun Nag (Subarnarekha, Calcutta, 1991) p 65.

6. Ranabir Roy Choudhury (ed.), *Glimpses of Old Calcutta (Period 1836-1850)* (Nachiketa Publications, Bombay, 1978) p 48.

7. Kaliprasanna Singha, *Hutom Pnyachar Naksha*, ed. Arun Nag (Subarnarekha, Calcutta, 1991) p 65.

8. Kaliprasanna Singha, *Hutom Pnyachar Naksha*, ed. Arun Nag (Subarnarekha, Calcutta, 1991) Editor's note, p 70-71.

9. A man with the surname 'Singha'. The word in Bengali means lion.

10. Bimal Chandra Ghosh, *Durga Puja Sekal Theke Ekal* (Ramkrishna Vivekananda Institute of Research and Culture, Calcutta, 1986) p 256.
11. Kaliprasanna Singha, *Hutom Pnyachar Naksha*, ed. Arun Nag (Subarnarekha, Calcutta, 1991) Editor's note, p 72.
12. "Kathamo Chhere Juddhey", *Ajkal*, October 15, 1993.
13. "Baroari pujor kharach kibhabe barchhey", *Saptahik Bartaman*, September 24, 1994.
14. Bimal Chandra Ghosh, *Durga Puja Sekal Theke Ekal* (Ramkrishna Vivekananda Institute of Research and Culture, Calcutta, 1986) p 143.
15. Sisir Kumar Bose and Birendra Nath Sinha (ed.), *Netaji: A Pictorial Biography* (Ananda Publishers, Calcutta, 1984), p 28.
16. Sunil Gangopadhyay, "Ek Jibone Eto Rupantar", *Anandabazar Patrika*, October 22, 1993.
17. Jibantara Haldar, *Banglar Prosiddha Anushilan Samitir Sankhipta Itihas* (Shakti Press, Calcutta, 1965) p 20.
18. "Pujor Smriti", *Bartaman*, October 16, 1993.
19. "Maharashtra O Kolkatar Pujo", *Anandabazar Patrika*, October 15, 1993.
20. Bimal Chandra Ghosh, *Durga Puja Sekal Theke Ekal* (Ramkrishna Vivekananda Institute of Research and Culture, Calcutta, 1986) p 274.
21. "Heri Je Muroti", *Anandabazar Patrika*, October 19, 1985.
22. "Ekhon Ar Chanda Sadhar Chol Nei", *Anandabazar Patrika*, September 30, 1985.

Chapter 5

1. The holy journey of Lord Jagannath in his chariot for a sea-bath in June-July.
2. "Debuttar" denotes property endowed for defraying the cost of worshipping a deity. "Deb" in Sanskrit means god.
3. Krishna Dutta, *Calcutta: A Cultural and Literary History* (Lotus Collection, Roli Books: New Delhi, 2003) p 52.
4. See 1.

5. Other communities are known to actively participate in the Puja, to the extent of being an integral part of the organisation. Such instances are visible in both the city and the districts. Behind New Market in Calcutta, a puja is held for over 30 years within shouting distance of a masjid. Not only do Muslim youths of the locality share the burden of work, they occupy important positions in the executive committee as well. "There is a rule that no puja can be performed within 200 feet of a masjid. But this has never been a problem in our case," the secretary of the committee affirms. There are similar instances of members of the two communities organising Durga Puja together in other corners of the state, including in a traditional Muslim base like the Murshidabad district.

6. Chandannagore, originally a French colony on the Hooghly not far from Calcutta, had always been famous for the wonderful illuminations conceived and executed for its Jagaddhatri Puja, Jagaddhatri being another name of Durga, though the two Pujas are not the same. Its technicians gradually acquired a new clientele in the form of the big-spending organisers of metropolitan Pujas. The most impressive display of lights might still be reserved for Kali Puja or Diwali—but Durga Puja soon became a close contender.

7. "Budget on the rise, exports fall", *The Telegraph*, October 9, 1994.

8. "If it's all about money, so be it", *The Telegraph*, September 20, 2003. Seventy crore equals 700 million.

9. "If it's all about money, so be it", *The Telegraph*, September 20, 2003. Three hundred and fifty crore equals 3.5 billion.

10. "Pujobazar special", *Anandabazar Patrika*, October 13, 1985.

11. Some poems and a tribute to the Goddess were included in the 2nd Kartik, 1280 (1873), number of the weekly *Madhyanho*. In 1913 (1320) the Kartik number of the monthy *Bharatbarsha* had contributions from the best writers of the time. In 1925, the monthly *Basumati* dedicated its autumn edition to Durga

Puja. In 1922, *Anandabazar Patrika* had six pages of Puja writings. But the first time that a Puja special came out in a separate magazine form was the 1926 edition of *Anandabazar Patrika*. In the same year, *Bharati* also brought out its golden jubilee edition as a Puja special, priced at Re 1. ("Sharad Sankhya", *Anandabazar Patrika*, October 13, 2002).

12. "Pujosankhyar sekal ar ekal", *Anandabazar Patrika*, September 30, 1985.

13. Ranabir Ray Choudhury (ed.), *Early Calcutta Advertisements (1875-1925)* (Nachiketa Publications, Bombay, 1992) p 40.

14. Ranabir Ray Choudhury (ed.), *Early Calcutta Advertisements (1875-1925)* (Nachiketa Publications, Bombay, 1992) p 48.

15. Ranabir Ray Choudhury (ed.), *Early Calcutta Advertisements (1875-1925)* (Nachiketa Publications, Bombay, 1992) p 185.

16. Geoffrey Moorhouse, *Calcutta* (Weidenfeld and Nicolson, London, 1971) p 198.

17. *Anandabazar Patrika*, September 30, 1985.

18. "Baroari pujor kharach kibhabe barchhey", *Saptahik Bartaman*, September 24, 1994.

19. "Megh mathay niye nirapottar byuha bhengei anandoplabon", *Anandabazar Patrika*, October 14, 2002.

20. Refer to Chapter IV.

21. Bimal Chandra Ghosh, *Durga Puja Sekal Theke Ekal* (Ramkrishna Vivekananda Institute of Research and Culture, Calcutta, 1986) p 222.

22. Bimal Chandra Ghosh, *Durga Puja Sekal Theke Ekal* (Ramkrishna Vivekananda Institute of Research and Culture, Calcutta, 1986) p 212.

23. Bimal Chandra Ghosh, *Durga Puja Sekal Theke Ekal* (Ramkrishna Vivekananda Institute of Research and Culture, Calcutta, 1986) p 217.

24. "Durga in land of dragon people", *The Telegraph*, September 22, 2004.

25. Madangopal Mukhopadhyay, "Bideshey Bangalider Durgapujo" in Sunil Gangopadhyay (ed.), *Smarak Grantha*, Biswabanga

Sammelan Millennium Committee (Ananda Publishers, Calcutta, 1999) p 301.

26. Bimal Chandra Ghosh, *Durga Puja Sekal Theke Ekal* (Ramkrishna Vivekananda Institute of Research and Culture, Calcutta, 1986) p 234.

27. Mohun Bagan and East Bengal are two sports clubs that are traditional rivals on the football field. For close to a century now, supporters have fixed their loyalties depending on which side of undivided Bengal their roots were in. While the people of West Bengal supported Mohun Bagan, those from the eastern side (now Bangladesh) rooted for East Bengal. The loyalties are not that pronounced—nor divided rigidly along boundary lines—in the present generation.

Conclusion

1. Chidananda Dasgupta, "Succour for the Downhearted", *The Telegraph*, October 16, 1993.

Glossary

Aalta: A red dye applied to the borders of women's feet

Aarati: The ritual of greeting a deity

Bel: Woodapple tree

Bodhan: Awakening

Chakshudan: Gift of eyes

Devipaksha: The divine fortnight in autumn

Dhakis: Players of drums called dhak

Diya: Lamp

Ghot: A pot full of holy water representing the god's or goddess' spiritual presence

Hom: Sacrificial fire

Kanshor-ghonta: A percussion instrument comprising a bell metal plate and a stick

Kshirod Sagar: The mythical sea of milk

Kirtan: A genre of devotional songs

Krittikas: Demigoddesses

Kumari: Virgin

Mahalaya: The great festival at home

Mahasnan: The great bath

Mantra: Incantations

Nabapatrika: A collection of nine branches of plants, kept to the right of Ganesha during the worship of Durga

Paan:	Betel leaf
Pandal:	A bamboo structure supporting lengths of cloth and woodwork
Paramatma:	The Supreme Being
Parijat:	The heavenly flower
Pitritarpan:	Sacrament of offering tribute to forefathers
Prasaad:	Food rendered sacred by being offered first to the deity
Pranaam:	A gesture of reverence
Pushpanjali:	Floral offering
Saaj:	Decoration
Sandhi puja:	Worship at the conjunction of Days VIII and IX of Devipaksha
Sattvaguna:	Sublime quality of one's spirit
Shakambhari:	Nourisher of herbs
Siddhi:	Success. Also the name of an intoxicant
Sindur khela:	Vermilion festival
Thakurdalan:	A hall for worship open to the sky with a covered raised platform at one end on which the idol is placed
Tithi:	Prescribed auspicious moment in the almanac. In ancient astronomical terms, a tithi is completed when the longitude of the moon gains exactly 12 degrees or its mutiple on that of the sun
Vak:	Speech
Veena:	Stringed musical instrument, found in Saraswati's hand
Vijaya Dashami:	The victorious tenth day of Debipaksha
Vrat:	Ritualistic observances prescribed for a period to fulfil a desire
Yagna:	Elaborate ritual of sacrifice to the gods

Bibliography

Anita Agnihotri, *Kolkatar Protimashilpira* (Ananda Publishers, Calcutta, 2001)

Anjan Mitra, *Kolkata O Durgapujo* (Ananda Publishers, Calcutta, 2003)

Bimal Chandra Ghosh, *Durga Puja Sekal Theke Ekal* (Ramkrishna Vivekananda Institute of Research and Culture, Calcutta, 1986)

Binoy Ghosh, *Kolkata Shohorer Itibritto* (Bak Sahitya, Calcutta, 1975)

Binoy Ghosh, *Paschimbanger Sanskriti,* Vol 2 (Prakash Bhavan, Calcutta, 1978)

Geoffrey Moorhouse, *Calcutta* (Weidenfeld and Nicolson, London, 1971)

Hansanarayan Bhattacharya, *Hinduder Debdebir Udbhab O Kromobikash* Vol 2 (Pharma KLM, Calcutta, 1978)

Hansanarayan Bhattacharya, *Hinduder Debdebir Udbhab O Kromobikash* Vol 3 (Pharma KLM, Calcutta, 1980)

Haripada Acharya, *Mahalaya Theke Bijoya* (Shree Ramkrishna Mission Ashram, Narendrapur, 1991)

Harisadhan Mukhopadhyay, *Kolikata Sekaler O Ekaler* (PM Bakchi and Co., Calcutta, 1991)

Jaya Chaliha and Bunny Gupta, "Durga Puja in Calcutta", in Sukanta Chaudhuri ed. *The Living City*, Vol 2 (Oxford University Press, Calcutta, 1990)

Kajal Mitra, *Kaley Kaley Kolkata* (Deer Prakashan, Calcutta, 1981)

Kaliprasanna Singha, *Hutom Pnyachar Naksha*, ed. Arun Nag (Subarnarekha, Calcutta, 1991)

Krishna Dutta, *Calcutta: A Cultural and Literary History* (Lotus Collection, Roli Books: New Delhi, 2003)

Nirmal Kar, *Banglar Durgotsab* (Nil Prakashan, Calcutta, 1999)

P.C. Bagchi (ed.), *The Second City of the Empire: The 25th Session of the Indian Science Association* (Calcutta, 1938)

Prankrishna Dutta, *Kolikatar Itibritto O Onyanno Rachana* (Pushtak Bipani, Calcutta, 1991)

P. Thankappan Nair (ed.), *Calcutta in the 19th Century* (Pharma KLM, Calcutta, 1989)

Purnendu Pattrea, *Ek Je Chilo Kolkata* (Protikkhan Publications, Calcutta, 1985)

Purba Sengupta, *Durga Rupey Rupantarey* (Mitra O Ghosh Publishers, Calcutta, 1998)

Ranabir Ray Choudhury (ed.), *Glimpses of Old Calcutta (Period 1836-1850)* (Nachiketa Publications, Bombay, 1978)

Ranabir Ray Choudhury (ed.), *Early Calcutta Advertisements (1875-1925)* (Nachiketa Publications, Bombay, 1992)

Shripantho, *Smritir Pujo* (Punoshcho, Calcutta, 2003)

Sukumari Bhattacharji, *Legends of Devi* (Disha Books, Orient Longman: Mumbai, 1998)

Sunil Gangopadhyay (ed.), *Smarak Grantha*, Biswabanga Sammelan Millennium Committee (Ananda Publishers, Calcutta, 1999)

Swami Prajnanananda, *Mahishasuramardini-Durga* (Shree Ramkrishna Vedanta Math, Calcutta, 1990)

Subodh Kapoor (ed.), *The Hindus: Encyclopaedia of Hinduism* (Cosmo Publications, Delhi, 2000)

Upendrakishore Roychowdhury, *Upendrakishorer Rachanasanggraha* (Akhil Bharat Janashiksha Prachar Samiti, Calcutta)

Vettam Mani, *Puranic Encyclopaedia* (Motilal Banarsidass, Delhi, 1975)

Information about the newspaper articles used have been mentioned in the notes to the chapters.